Gendered Justice?

FEMINIST DEVELOPMENTS IN VIOLENCE AND ABUSE

Series Editors: Dr Hannah Bows, Durham University (UK) and Professor Nicole Westmarland, Durham University (UK)

Feminist Developments in Violence and Abuse provides a feminist forum for academic work that pushes forward existing knowledge around violence and abuse, informing policy and practice, with the overarching objective of contributing towards ending violence and abuse within our society. The series enables academics, practitioners, policymakers, and professionals to continually build and explore their understanding of the dynamics, from the micro to the macro level, that are driving violence and abuse. The study of abuse and violence has a large scope for co-producing research, and this series is a home for research involving a broad range of stakeholders; particularly those working in grassroots domestic and sexual violence organisations, police, prosecutors, lawyers, campaign groups, and housing and victim services. As violence and abuse research reaches across disciplinary boundaries, the series has an interdisciplinary scope with research impact at the heart.

Available Volumes:

Victims' Experiences of the Criminal Justice Response to Domestic Abuse: Beyond Glass Walls
Emma Forbes

Understanding and Responding to Economic Abuse
Nicola Sharp-Jeffs

Rape Myths: Understanding, Assessing, and Preventing
Sofia Persson and Katie Dhingra

Forthcoming Volumes:

'Rough Sex' and the Criminal Law: Global Perspectives
Hannah Bows and Jonathan Herring

Not Your Usual Suspect: Older Offenders of Violence and Abuse
Hannah Bows

Gendered Justice? How Women's Attempts to Cope With, Survive, or Escape Domestic Abuse Can Drive Them into Crime

BY

JO ROBERTS
University of South Wales, UK

United Kingdom – North America – Japan – India – Malaysia – China

Emerald Publishing Limited
Emerald Publishing, Floor 5, Northspring, 21-23 Wellington Street, Leeds LS1 4DL.

First edition 2022

Copyright © 2022 Jo Roberts.
Published under exclusive licence by Emerald Publishing Limited.

British Library Cataloguing in Publication Data
A catalogue record for this book is available from the British Library

ISBN: 978-1-80262-070-2 (Print)
ISBN: 978-1-80262-069-6 (Online)
ISBN: 978-1-80262-071-9 (Epub)
ISBN: 978-1-80262-072-6 (Paperback)

INVESTOR IN PEOPLE

Contents

About the Author

Dr Jo Roberts is a Lecturer in Criminology and Criminal Justice whose research interests include violence against women and girls (specifically domestic abuse), and women's pathways into the criminal justice system. She has worked in the fields of domestic abuse prevention and women's offending for the last 15 years, within both research and policy-based roles. This experience has fuelled her desire to conduct research which draws upon women's own words and experiences, amplifies women's voices, has real-world implications and, as a result, helps inform criminal justice policy and practice.

Acknowledgements

This book is dedicated to the brave and selfless women who shared their stories with me and afforded me the privilege of listening to them. It should be recognised that their recollection of often extremely traumatic experiences would have taken both honesty and strength. Importantly it is the women's perspectives and their own words which provide the foundations for the book and without their involvement neither the research nor this book would have been possible.

I am grateful for the support and encouragement I received from the Wales Probation Trust and in particular for those members of staff that, despite their already overwhelming workloads, generously gave their time and input without which the fieldwork would not have been possible. Many of the staff that took part in, or otherwise supported, the study had themselves been subjected to domestic abuse and therefore understood the importance of the research on a deeply personal level. The experiences of the staff members reflect the wide reach of domestic abuse where women of all ages, classes, ethnicities, and backgrounds can be affected, emphasising the need for everyone to work together to eradicate all forms of violence against women.

I am also forever indebted to the Department of Criminology at the University of Leicester who saw the potential both in me and my ideas. I couldn't be more grateful for the funding I was awarded as I would not have been able to undertake my doctoral studies if it weren't for this financial support. I would also like to personally thank my supervisor, Dr Sarah Hodgkinson, by acknowledging the unrelenting support and insight that she provided throughout my studies and has continued to do so long after.

My sister deserves special mention with an understanding that words cannot do justice to her unwavering support, motivation, and always helpful contributions. The belief she has shown in me has never relented even when I had none.

The accounts included within this book are the reflections of women's real-life experiences and lives and their recollections add further gravity to the sentiment that the personal is political. The feminist approach of the study was pivotal as it reinforces the unremitting importance of raising women's voices and always attempting to impact upon the real word ensuring that women's experiences are acknowledged and addressed both within policy and practice.

Summary

The presence of domestic abuse victimisation in the histories or backgrounds of women who come into contact with the criminal justice system has been well documented. Yet despite recognition that a link between a woman's victimisation and her involvement in crime exists the relationship between the two is still not well understood. Drawing on the experiences of women serving community-based sentences, all of whom had experienced domestic abuse, this book describes how a woman's involvement in crime can manifest as a by-product of her attempts to cope with, escape, or survive domestic abuse. Placing women's voices at the very centre of the discourse this book will present a range of ways in which women's experiences of domestic abuse have contributed to their pathways into crime. Much of the existing literature in this area has focussed upon crimes committed by women with, for, or against their abusive partners. This book, based upon the findings of the first UK based research of its kind, will instead demonstrate how a woman's involvement in crime can occur in a much broader context, including without women's abusers being present, after the abusive relationship has ended, or even years after the abuse has ceased yet the women's actions can still be attributed to their experiences of domestic abuse. This book will also explore how a woman's experience of domestic abuse can impact her ability to carry out her sentence as well as provide examples of perpetrators of domestic abuse employing the criminal justice system as yet another weapon of abuse. Finally, drawing upon supplementary interviews undertaken with staff working in probation, this book will also examine further ways that a woman's experience of domestic abuse can impact upon her contact with the criminal justice system, raising important matters related to women's supervision and support. Given that the foundations of the book are built upon women's real-life experiences, which have real-world implications, it is important to reflect on these; therefore, the book will conclude by presenting a range of recommendations and implications for both policy and practice in the field of criminal justice.

Gendered Justice? How Women's Attempts to Cope With, Survive, or Escape Domestic Abuse Can Drive Them into Crime, 1–1
Copyright © 2022 by Jo Roberts
Published under exclusive licence by Emerald Publishing Limited
doi:10.1108/978-1-80262-069-620221001

Chapter 1

Women and Domestic Abuse

I've been tortured, I've had my hair set on fire ... I've had real bad things happen to me, I've had my jaw broken [and] I've had my nose bust 3 times. (Charlie)

I weren't allowed friends, weren't allowed out, couldn't go shopping on my own. I could walk to the school and back and that's about it. Never, never went out ... when I worked at the school and I worked with [my abusive partner's] sister in law, I was having an affair with his brother, his sister-in-law, everybody! And he said how can you work in the school you're too thick! ... if I spoke to anybody [he'd say to me] 'I don't want you speaking to [them]'.... (Grace)

All of the women who were interviewed for the study which is outlined in this book had come into contact with the criminal justice system (CJS) and had been subjected to domestic abuse. The quotations above provide just a small insight into the varying types of violence and abuse the women who participated in the study had experienced. For the vast majority of the women who were interviewed for the research they recalled how their experiences of violence and abuse had, in some way, influenced or contributed to their pathways into crime. Before exploring the perspectives and accounts of the brave women who took part in the study, it is first important to understand what domestic abuse is, who is affected by it, how prevalent it is, and the effects it can have on women's lives.

Violence Against Women and Girls

Violence against women and girls is a global epidemic affecting millions of women and girls across all continents, cultures, religions, classes, ages, and ethnicities. Data collected over a period of 10 years by the World Health Organisation (WHO) from across 161 countries and areas estimate that globally approximately 30 percent of women, that is 1 in every 3, have been subjected to physical and/or sexual abuse perpetrated either by an intimate partner or a non-intimate partner (WHO, 2021). Furthermore, WHO (2021) data also illustrate that worldwide

Gendered Justice? How Women's Attempts to Cope With, Survive, or Escape Domestic Abuse Can Drive Them into Crime, 3–9
Copyright © 2022 by Jo Roberts
Published under exclusive licence by Emerald Publishing Limited
doi:10.1108/978-1-80262-069-620221002

27 percent of women, that is, almost one-third of all women aged 15–49, have reported being subjected to physical and/ or sexual abuse by an intimate partner. Violence against women is defined by the United Nations as:

> any act of gender-based violence that results in, or is likely to result in, physical, sexual, or mental harm or suffering to women, including threats of such acts, coercion or arbitrary deprivation of liberty, whether occurring in public or in private life. (WHO, 2021)

Importantly, the WHO recognise that intimate partner violence (IPV), that is violence perpetrated against a woman by her intimate partner, is not only a significant violation of a woman's human rights but also constitutes a major public health concern (WHO, 2021). The WHO (2021) also note that across the world around 38 percent of all murders of women are committed by their intimate partners, demonstrating the lethality of violence against women.

Domestic Abuse

Domestic abuse is part of the continuum of violence against women and is similar to IPV but extends further by recognising that perpetrators of domestic abuse can include a wide range of family members (including both immediate and/or distant family). Therefore, domestic abuse as a term also encapsulates both IPV and adolescent to parent violence (APV). The term domestic abuse, as opposed to domestic violence, has been employed throughout the study and this book as this indicates that domestic abuse is not limited to physical abuse alone and instead encompasses a broad range of tactics employed by abuse perpetrators including sexual, financial, and psychological/emotional abuse. Lastly, utilising the definition of domestic abuse also allows for the recognition of coercive and controlling behaviours which often comprise an integral dynamic of domestic abuse.

The specific definition of domestic abuse that was current at the time of the fieldwork for the study was taken from the Home Office (2013) and was included in the UK Government domestic violence and abuse guidance. Significantly, the UK definition of domestic abuse was expanded further during the course of the research when Stark's (2007) concept of coercive control was incorporated into it in March 2013. The definition used throughout this book, therefore, defines domestic abuse as:

> any incident or pattern of incidents of controlling, coercive, threatening behaviour, violence or abuse between those aged 16 or over who are, or have been, intimate partners or family members regardless of gender or sexuality. The abuse can encompass, but is not limited to: psychological, physical, sexual, financial, emotional …. (Home Office, 2013, n.p.)

Stark's (2007) concept of coercive control is heavily referenced throughout this book and aligns closely with the theoretical positioning of the research, as it describes a model of abusive behaviours, tactics, and strategies that are predominantly employed by men and used to dominate women within their personal lives. Stark's (2007) model of coercive control interweaves repeated physical violence (although physical violence is not always present in abusive relationships) with tactics of sexual degradation, intimidation, isolation, and control. Notably, Stark (2007) points to the foundations of coercive control as originating in the micro processes of relationships and within the dynamics of everyday existence whilst acknowledging the impact of structures which reinforce and sustain women's subordination at both a societal and individual level. Therefore, coercive control, as Stark describes it, constitutes an extremely personal form of abuse that is reinforced by, and originally derives from, a background of patriarchal society's sexual discrimination and female subordination. Stark's theories of coercive control and the recognition of how both macro and micro processes combine to facilitate a woman's experience of abuse provided an important foundation to the theoretical and methodological positioning of this research, influencing the way in which the research was approached and conducted.[1]

There are two further elements of Stark's (2007) concept of coercive control that were important for this study; these were his identification of both the gendered nature and individualised dimensions of this type of abuse, as he describes:

> Its particularity lies in its aim – to usurp and master a partner's subjectivity – in its scope of its deployment, its individualised and personal dimensions, and its focus on imposing sex stereotypes in everyday life. The result is a condition of unfreedom ... that is 'gendered' in its construction, delivery and consequence. (Stark, 2007, p. 205)

As Stark (2007) demonstrates it is the individual knowledge that each perpetrator holds about his victim, for example, regarding their day-to-day activities, their routine, behaviours, personal fears and medical problems, that enables the targeted and highly personal dynamics of coercive control. Therefore, the foundations of coercive control are not only built upon the extremely personal knowledge that each perpetrator has of his victim but also the privileged access that he has to them (Stark, 2007) and this deeply personal knowledge of the victim is employed as a key dynamic of the abuse. Furthermore, these tactics are employed within a private and often unmonitored sphere, leaving the victim with little or no room for escape. It was this specific element of coercive control that was integral in the framing of the research outlined in this book as this helped to facilitate a better understanding of how women's experiences of domestic abuse may affect their pathways into crime, via examining the nuances and subjective nature of abuse and coercive control, and in particular, the actions women take to cope with, respond to, and survive it.

A final resource that was drawn upon for the study was the Duluth Model and in particular the Duluth Power and Control Wheel (Domestic Abuse Intervention

---

[1]Further information relating to this can be found in Appendix A.

Programmes, 2011). The Power and Control Wheel is a resource that is frequently referenced by those working in the field of domestic abuse as it depicts some of the common strategies employed by perpetrators of domestic abuse which includes threats, intimidation, isolation, undermining victims' autonomy, as well as tactics involving victims' children. As these tactics demonstrate the significance of the Power and Control Wheel lies in its broad categorisations of behaviours and actions which are employed by perpetrators of domestic abuse, many of which are unrelated to physical violence. Furthermore, this resource also emphasises the repeat nature[2] of abuse which comprises '… part of a *pattern* of behaviours rather than isolated incidents of abuse[3] or cyclical explosions of pent-up anger, frustration, or painful feelings' (Domestic Violence Information Manual, 1993, n.p., emphasis added). It is, however, important to recognise the limitations of this resource as the Power and Control model is fundamentally based on Western cultural understandings of domestic abuse and does not (and is not meant) to provide a definitive or exhaustive list of behaviours that can be employed within all domestic abuse situations (Harne and Radford, 2008).

When discussing definitions of domestic abuse, it is also helpful to mention that in April 2021 the *Domestic Abuse Act* (2021) received royal assent in England.[4] This Act created a new statutory definition of domestic abuse which recognises that domestic abuse does not simply consist of physical violence but includes controlling and threatening behaviours as well as economic, psychological, and emotional abuse (*Domestic Abuse Act, 2021*). Furthermore, the new Act acknowledges that children do not simply witness domestic abuse recognising them as victims in their own right.

The Gendered Nature of Domestic Abuse

Despite variation across countries and cultures relating to the form domestic abuse may take (Krug et al., 2002), one clear pattern emerges: domestic abuse is distinctly gendered in its nature. It is well understood that women are disproportionately the victims of domestic abuse and that men are overwhelmingly the perpetrators (Office for National Statistics or ONS, 2021b, 2021c; Her Majesty's Inspectorate of Constabulary and Fire and Rescue Services or HMICFRS, 2019; Refuge, 2014; Chaplin et al., 2011). This recognition led the WHO (2002), the

---

[2]The repeat nature of domestic abuse perpetration is highly significant as HMICFRS (2019, p. 16) noted that: 'victims of domestic abuse are more likely to be repeat victims than are victims of any other crime type'.

[3]Hence there is also some crossover with Stark's coercive control with regard to this aspect of the Duluth definition.

[4]Prior to the *Domestic Abuse Act* (2021) there was already existing legislation in Wales – the *Violence against Women, Domestic Abuse and Sexual Violence (Wales) Act* (2015). As a consequence of the devolved natures of the Scottish, Welsh, and Northern Irish Governments the majority of provisions in the 2021 Act mainly relate to England and Wales, or England only and some relate to devolved matters in Scotland and Northern Ireland (Home Office, 2021).

United Nations (UN) (United Nations Declaration on the Elimination of Violence against Women, 1993) and the Council of Europe (2011) to define domestic abuse as a gender-based phenomenon.

Elaborating further on the gendered nature of domestic abuse; being female is the single most significant risk factor (ONS, 2021b, 2021c; SafeLives, 2021; Women's Aid, 2021a; HMICFRS, 2019; Refuge, 2014) and domestic abuse is the most prevalent crime where women are the victims (HMIC, 2014; Chaplin et al., 2011; HM Government 2010a, 2010b). Police data further highlight the gendered nature of domestic abuse victimisation as during the year ending March 2021 records kept by 26 police forces indicated that in 73 percent of all domestic abuse related crime cases the victims were female (ONS, 2021c). Drawing upon data from the Crime Survey for England and Wales (CSEW) the gendered patterns of domestic abuse victimisation are also illustrated. The CSEW estimates that of those who completed the survey, (all of whom were aged between 16 and 74), 2.3 million reported experience of domestic abuse and this figure was divided into 1.6 million women and 757,000 men (ONS, 2020b)[5]. Furthermore, recent Crown Prosecution Service (CPS) data indicated, where the sex of the complainant was recorded, that in 82.5 percent of domestic abuse cases the victims were female, compared with 17.5 percent of cases which involved male victims (CPS, 2019)[6]. CPS data relating to the sex of the defendant, where this was captured, demonstrates that of the 78,624 individuals prosecuted for domestic abuse offences 92.1 percent were men and 7.9 percent were women (CPS, 2019). Alongside this, further research has identified that perpetrators of domestic abuse are predominantly male (Hester, 2013). Consequently, both the CPS and other sources of data demonstrate that women do not only comprise the largest proportion of victims of domestic abuse but indicate that men are far more likely to perpetrate domestic abuse, therefore, compounding the notion that domestic abuse is gendered – both in its victimisation *and* perpetration.

At this point it is of course necessary to reference some of the problems associated with domestic abuse statistics and their validity, specifically in regard to the production and use of CJS data or official statistics. One significant issue encountered is the general underreporting of domestic abuse across all data sources (Dutton, 2006; Walby and Allen, 2004; Felson et al., 2002) which reflect the myriad of barriers women face when considering making a disclosure (Gracia, 2004). The lack of reporting to the police in particular is highlighted by the CSEW as their data indicates that only 18 percent of the women who reported

---

[5]Due to the COVID-19 pandemic the face-to-face CSEW was suspended and subsequently conducted over the telephone. As a result of the change in data collection method, there were concerns related to safeguarding and risk and subsequently, the domestic abuse questions were dropped from the questionnaire. Therefore, there are no domestic abuse estimates available from the CSEW for the year ending March 2021 (ONS, 2021c).

[6]Just to note that in some cases the sex of the complainant or defendant was not recorded which explains why the data does not total 100 percent.

having experienced domestic abuse in the year ending March 2018 had actually reported their experiences to the police (taken from Women's Aid, 2021b). These distinct levels of underreporting have led to the employment of the term 'iceberg' when referring to cases of domestic abuse as this describes the small numbers of incidents of domestic abuse that are actually captured by official statistics (Gracia, 2004). Despite significant levels of underreporting, the prevalence of domestic abuse is extremely concerning as the Police in England and Wales, on average, receive over 100 calls every hour which relate to domestic abuse (HMIC, 2015).

A further issue with criminal justice data specifically relates to the legal positioning of domestic abuse as an offence category. Although domestic abuse is a crime, there is an absence of a discrete offence of 'domestic abuse' within the law which causes difficulties when attempting to acquire domestic abuse data from recorded crime sources as the categorisations of offences will generally reflect the legal definitions (Thompson, 2010). Despite the problems associated with the reliability of domestic abuse statistics, all available data demonstrate that large numbers of women are affected by domestic abuse, that domestic abuse is prevalent across England and Wales, and that it is gendered in its nature.

To elaborate on the gendered dynamics of domestic abuse; whilst both men and women can be subjected to domestic abuse, as Women's Aid (2021a) note there are significant differences in how men and women experience it where these differences relate to the prevalence, severity, and impact. Moreover, the notion that domestic abuse exists within, and is reinforced by, gendered societal structures also contributes to its gendered nature, and as a result, women are more likely to experience domestic abuse (ONS, 2020a). When examining prevalence and incidents evidence shows that women, rather than men, are more likely to be subjected to much higher rates of repeat victimisation where incidents are perpetrated by the same person, therefore, the repetition itself is gendered (Walby and Towers, 2018, 2017). Walby and Towers (2017), drawing upon their own research, demonstrate how repeat victimisation directly relates to gender. They found that in regard to cases where victims are categorised as high-frequency (those who had been subjected to 10 or more domestic abuse crimes in a year) 83 percent of these victims were women. The disparity between how men and women experience domestic abuse is also exemplified by data that highlights how women are far more likely than men to be seriously injured or killed as a result of domestic abuse (Smith, 2021; Women's Aid, 2021a; Walby and Allen, 2004).

Multi-Agency Risk Assessment Conferences (MARACs) are regular meetings where a range of professionals meet to discuss how to help high-risk victims of domestic abuse. Only those who have been assessed to be within the top 10 percent of highest risk victims are discussed at MARAC and here risk refers to risk of serious harm or homicide (Standing Together, 2021). At these conferences information is shared between representatives of local police, health, child protection, housing practitioners, Independent Domestic Violence Advisors (IDVAs) and other specialists from both the statutory and voluntary sectors. Data collected from MARACs also corroborate the assertion that women are more likely to be higher risk victims of domestic abuse. MARAC data from the year ending

March 2021 indicate that of the 107,885 cases that were discussed at MARACs in England and Wales in 93.9 percent of the cases the victims were women (Safe Lives, 2021b). When examining homicide data, as has been indicated earlier, again it is women that are most likely to be at risk of murder committed within the context of domestic abuse. In the UK, the 10-year Femicide Census revealed that, on average, a woman is killed by a current or former partner every four days (Smith, 2021). Homicide figures collected for the Home Office Homicide Index also corroborate the point made by Women's Aid regarding how women are more likely to be murdered as a result of domestic abuse, as in the year ending March 2020 76 percent of domestic homicide victims were women (ONS, 2021a).

Finally, the gendered nature of domestic abuse is further evidenced by research which found that in comparison to men that are subjected to domestic abuse women are more likely to experience greater levels of fear (Dobash and Dobash, 2004; Hester, 2013; Myhill, 2015, 2017). In summary, the gendered nature of domestic abuse is clearly illustrated by a vast range of data. Before examining the impact of a woman's experience of domestic abuse on her pathway into crime, it is also helpful to explore how women's gendered experiences impact on women's wider involvement in crime and their criminalisation.

Chapter 2

Women and Crime: Situating Women's Offending within a Gendered Context

> Women account for a minority of all those coming into contact with criminal justice agencies, and their specific circumstances and needs are often overlooked or misunderstood by a system which has largely developed in response to men's offending profile and behaviour. Most women who enter custody under sentence serve short prison sentences for petty but sometimes persistent offending, and many have themselves been victims of domestic violence and sexual abuse. (Earle et al., 2014, p. 1)

It has long been argued that traditional, mainstream criminology is androcentric or, in other words, historically speaking criminological theory has largely been produced by men and has focussed on the activities and perspectives of men (Silvestri, 2016; Becker and McCorkel, 2011; Stanley and Wise, 1990; Heidensohn, 1985). As a result, until the late 1960s and early 1970s, the discipline had neglected to consider gender as a concept or view crime as a gendered activity (Becker and McCorkel, 2011). In response to this, predominantly feminist academics (see, e.g., Gelsthorpe and Morris, 1990; Carlen, 1988; Heidensohn, 1985, 1989) began to focus solely on women's involvement in crime, and their experiences in the CJS. As a result, they identified marked differences in the behaviours of women and men, demonstrating how gender should be considered a significant variable when exploring crime. Subsequently, criminologists have labelled the differences between men's and women's involvement in crime the 'sex-crime ratio' (see Heidensohn and Gelsthorpe, 2007, p. 391) or alternatively, the 'gender-gap' in offending (see Becker and McCorkel, 2011, p. 79).

Before attempting to better understand the reasons behind women's offending and the pathways that women follow which can lead them into crime it is first important to examine what women's involvement in crime looks like and what differences exist between women's and men's offending behaviours. A vast body of literature has identified crime to be an overwhelmingly male activity (Silvestri, 2016) and there are distinct differences in the contact that men and women have

Gendered Justice? How Women's Attempts to Cope With, Survive,
or Escape Domestic Abuse Can Drive Them into Crime, 11–14
Copyright © 2022 by Jo Roberts
Published under exclusive licence by Emerald Publishing Limited
doi:10.1108/978-1-80262-069-620221003

with the CJS which includes notable variation in the extent, seriousness, and frequency of women's involvement in crime when compared to men. The available data, which refers to England and Wales, highlight that men are substantially over-represented within the CJS at all levels (MOJ, 2020). The first difference between men's and women's involvement in crime is that women commit far less crime than men (MOJ, 2020; Silvestri, 2016; Heidenson and Gelsthorpe, 2007; McIvor, 2007). This statement is corroborated by the numbers of arrests in England and Wales where the data recorded that 85 percent of all those arrested in 2019–2020 were men and this is a figure that has remained stable for the last 3 years (MOJ, 2020). The numbers of men and women who engage with liaison and diversion services[1] continue to reflect that it is men who are much more likely to come into contact with the CJS, as only 21 percent of 85,900 individuals that came into contact with these services were women (MOJ, 2020). Furthermore, MOJ (2020) data also highlight men's disproportionate involvement in criminal activity as in 2019 only 26 percent of individuals coming into contact with the CJS as offenders were women, compared with 74 percent that were male and these proportions have remained consistent for the past 5 years. When it comes to sentencing, again men comprise the majority of those being processed by the courts and in 2019 only 27 percent of the 1.07 million offenders sentenced were women (MOJ, 2020). When reviewing prison data, once more it is men that comprise the majority of those being sentenced to custody with the June 2019 figures indicating that 95 percent of the prison population were men compared to only 5 percent women (MOJ, 2020).

The aforementioned statistics provide clear indication that criminal activity is not gender-neutral and there are also marked differences in the types of crime that women and men commit (Heidensohn, 1996). This variation refers specifically to the seriousness of crimes committed where the perpetration of rape, homicide, and most violent crimes is predominantly male-dominated (ONS, 2021a; MOJ, 2020; Smith et al., 2011, 2012). Homicide data collected by the ONS (2021a) clearly indicate that, when compared with women, men are far more likely to perpetrate murder. During the year March 2019 until April 2020 a total of 179 men and only 8 women were convicted of homicide (ONS, 2021a). For the previous year the figures were significantly higher and men were convicted of 397 murders in the year from March 2018 to April 2019 compared with 31 women (ONS, 2021a).

Although women do, of course, commit a whole range of offences women's crimes tend to be concentrated in much lower level offences (Earle et al., 2014; Gelsthorpe, 2004). Once again this is corroborated by the available data, for example, MOJ (2020) statistics identified that in 2019 the most common offence for which women were convicted in England and Wales was TV Licence evasion.

---

[1]Liaison and diversion services are health-based services which engage with individuals coming into contact with the CJS as suspects, defendants, or offenders in order to identify mental health, learning disabilities, and substance use needs or other vulnerabilities.

TV Licence evasion accounted for 30 percent of the entire total of all women's criminal activities, when comparing this with men's patterns of offending this offence accounted for only 4 percent of men's total offending (MOJ, 2020). When reviewing the different offence groups the figures for 2019 illustrate that men's offending far outnumbered women in every single offence category (MOJ, 2020). In terms of the types of offences; women were most commonly prosecuted for fraud and theft offences, where women comprised 33 percent and 21 percent of individuals prosecuted in those areas respectively (MOJ, 2020). Men's prosecutions were, however, concentrated in the sexual offence and possession of weapon categories where 98 percent of those prosecuted for sexual offences and 93 percent prosecuted for weapons offences were men (MOJ, 2020).

Sentencing data also suggest that women commit less serious offences than men as the MOJ (2020) identified that consistently larger proportions of men receive custodial sentences whereas the larger proportion of women receive community-based sentences. Statistics on sentence length also arguably make comment on the seriousness/severity of crimes committed as in 2019, a higher proportion of women (50 percent of those who were given custodial sentences) were sentenced to 3 months or less compared with only 31 percent of all men who were sentenced (MOJ, 2020). When reviewing numbers of men and women being supervised by probation the pattern continues; in 2019 women comprised only 17 percent of individuals who were issued community orders compared with 83 percent who were men (MOJ, 2020). As seen in the custodial sentence data again, the MOJ (2020) data highlight how women were allocated to shorter community sentences than men.

Pathways into Crime

All of the available data indicate that gender can function as a predictor of CJS involvement where women make a very limited contribution to overall offending. Conclusively, criminological research combined with criminal justice data illustrates that 'women commit significantly less crime than men and the crime they commit is typically less serious, less violent, and less profitable' (Becker and McCorkel, 2011, p. 79). As a result of the profound differences between women's and men's involvement in crime and the disparities between their journeys into offending, some criminologists have called for better recognition and exploration of the 'gendered contexts and experiences…[which] underpin women's criminalisation …' (Segrave and Carlton, 2010, p. 287). Such experiences include particular life circumstances that are contoured by gender, an example of which is women's disproportionate experience of domestic and sexual abuse. Consequently, a growing body of literature contends that women follow specific 'pathways' into crime and these pathways are also distinctly gendered (Becker and McCorkel, 2011). As Becker and McCorkel (2011) note 'pathways' research asserts that the crime trajectories followed by men and women differ significantly and this is reflected both in *how much* women participate in crime and *how* they participate.

The importance of 'pathways' research is that it suggests that in order to understand the causes of women's criminality and criminalisation a 'whole-life' approach should be taken; a process which contextualises women's involvement in crime by considering women's life events (see Bloom et al., 2014). The significance of this suggestion is that one aspect of a woman's life events that has been empirically established as playing a significant role in pathways into offending is women's disproportionate experience of violence and trauma, and most specifically experience of domestic abuse.

The next chapter will summarise the wide range of literature that has begun to highlight the prevalence of domestic abuse victimisation within the histories and backgrounds of women who have come into contact with the CJS. It will include reference to both academic and policy-based literature and will include literature from the UK and across the world.

Chapter 3

Women's Pathways into Offending and Domestic Abuse: Does a Relationship Between the Two Exist Outside of a Simple Co-occurrence?

> There are many women in prison ... for whom prison is both disproportionate and inappropriate ... Large numbers have endured violent or sexual abuse ... [and have been] exploited by men [and/or] damaged by abuse. (Corston, 2007, p. i)

It has long been recognised both within academic and policy-based literature, that high proportions of women, who come into contact with the CJS have histories or backgrounds of abuse (Centre for Social Justice, 2018; Women in Prison, 2017; Prison Reform Trust, 2017a, 2017b; Women's Aid, 2011; Jones, 2008; Corston, 2007). Arguably one of the most pivotal publications to have drawn attention to the specific vulnerabilities of women who come into contact with the CJS was the Corston Report (2007). Unfortunately, it was the deaths of six women that occurred whilst they were in custody at HMP Styal that acted as a catalyst for this review bringing women's vulnerabilities into sharp focus and raising questions about the appropriateness of imprisonment for women. Although the review took place over a relatively short period of time, 6 months, Baroness Corston visited women's prisons, community centres, a medium secure women's hospital and engaged with over 250 individuals. Her investigation into the particular vulnerabilities of women who become involved in crime led Baroness Corston to state that she believed women's pathways into crime to be strongly connected to their vulnerabilities. In her report Baroness Corston (2007) divided women's vulnerability into three categories, the first of which was labelled 'domestic circumstances' and this included women's experience of domestic abuse (Corston, 2007, p. 2). The review generated increased recognition of the wide range of vulnerabilities of women in prison and revealed the prevalence of women in prison who have histories of abuse: 'Women with histories

Gendered Justice? How Women's Attempts to Cope With, Survive, or Escape Domestic Abuse Can Drive Them into Crime, 15–24
Copyright © 2022 by Jo Roberts
Published under exclusive licence by Emerald Publishing Limited
doi:10.1108/978-1-80262-069-620221004

of violence and abuse are overrepresented in the CJS and can be described as victims as well as offenders'. At the conclusion of her review, Baroness Corston (2007) stated that 'it comes as no surprise to me that relationship problems feature strongly in women's pathways into crime' (p. 19).

In the years since the Corston Report was published a growing body of literature has continued to draw attention to how women in the CJS are far more likely to have experienced domestic and/ or sexual violence than the wider female population (see, e.g., All Party Parliamentary Group – APPG on Women in the Penal System, 2020; Centre for Social Justice, 2018; Women in Prison, 2017; Prison Reform Trust, 2017a). In 2011, Women's Aid published *Supporting Women Offenders Who Have Experienced Domestic and Sexual Violence* the purpose of which was to provide guidance for professionals working with women who come into contact with the CJS to better respond to the needs of those women who have experienced domestic or sexual abuse. Women's Aid (2011) highlighted how, when compared to the general female population, experience of domestic abuse is significantly more common for women who come into contact with the CJS. Figures included in the Women's Aid (2011) report estimate that between 50 and 80 percent of women in prison have histories of domestic and/or sexual abuse. Importantly Women's Aid (2011) also drew attention to women who serve their sentences in the community as they recognised that these women will also have similar experiences to women in prison.

More recent policy-based publications have also provided an indication of the numbers of women involved with the CJS who have experienced domestic abuse. In 2015, the National Offender Management Service (NOMS) published *Better outcomes for female offenders* and using data drawn from OASys,[1] identified that 67 percent of women in prison or being supervised in the community by the National Probation Service (NPS) had reported experience of domestic abuse (NOMS, 2015). The figure was 61 percent for those women serving sentences in the community but being supervised by Community Rehabilitation Companies (NOMS, 2015). Notably, the NOMS (2015) data indicate that over half of the women in custody *and* being supervised in the community have reported domestic abuse victimisation. It is important to state, however, that the actual figures are likely to be much higher as with the NOMS data OASys assessments had not been completed with all women. In addition, not all women would necessarily report their experience of domestic abuse to a statutory agency for fear of what repercussions such a disclosure might have (such as having their children removed from their custody).

In 2017, 10 years after the Corston report was published, Women in Prison (WIP) published their own report, *Corston +10*, to reflect upon what progress

---

[1]OASys is the abbreviated term for the Offender Assessment System: a standardised process for the assessment of offenders that was developed jointly by the National Probation Service (NPS) and the Prison Service (Social Exclusion Task Force, 2009). OASys assessments measure the risks of re-offending, the needs of offenders, and other factors associated with the individual's offending.

been made in addressing the recommendations outlined by Baroness Corston. Unfortunately, WIP concluded that although the Corston report had placed the needs of women in the CJS at the forefront of the agenda, in its aftermath much of the work that had been promoted by the review had not been sustained (WIP, 2017). Consequently, WIP (2017) felt that there had been a considerable lack of progress in recognising the gendered needs of women who come into contact with the CJS. Pointedly WIP (2017, p. 3) emphasised that in order to achieve the changes needed to better support women who come into contact with the CJS:

> [...] it is vital for policy makers to recognise that criminal justice solutions alone are not sufficient to deal with offending ... What is required is a joined-up approach that takes into account the root causes of women's offending. This approach must encompass an understanding of the compelling opportunities for change that appropriate housing, mental health support, and gender-specific women's community support services can offer.

Later in 2017 the Prison Reform Trust (PRT) published a report which aimed to raise awareness of the links between women's experience of domestic abuse and their pathways into crime, demonstrating how domestic abuse can function as a driver to women's offending. In their report the PRT (2017a) highlighted the role that relationships can play in men's and women's offending where for men, relationships generally have a positive impact but for women, however, relationships can function as a risk factor as their experiences of coercive control, physical, emotional, and sexual abuse can have a direct impact on their pathways into crime. The PRT (2017a) provided clear examples of how women's experiences of domestic abuse can influence their involvement in crime including when women are coerced or become involved in criminal activities under duress, or where women may use violence to resist their abuse. They also noted how women's involvement in crime could be affected by specific forms of abuse, for example, when women commit financially motivated offences, such as benefit fraud, due to their experiences of financial abuse. The PRT (2017a, p. 9) concluded that:

> most women affected by domestic abuse do not commit offences, but the evidence suggests that for a majority of women in prison, the experience of domestic abuse has been a significant contributory factor.

Significantly, the relationship between women's experiences of domestic abuse and their involvement in crime was also recently referenced by the Ministry of Justice (MOJ). In 2018 the first ever *Female Offender Strategy* was published which acknowledged 'the major part that domestic abuse can play in female offending' (MOJ, 2018, p. 11). This document did not elaborate any further on the specifics of the role of domestic abuse but the MOJ did recognise the influence the multiple forms of abuse employed by perpetrators can have on women's offending including the use of coercive and controlling behaviours.

In 2019, the MOJ commissioned a review into women in the CJS entitled *The Importance of Strengthening Female Offenders' Family and other Relationships to Prevent Reoffending and Reduce Intergenerational Crime* (Farmer, 2019). This review, the second undertaken by Lord Farmer,[2] made reference to key differences between men and women who come into contact with the CJS:

> There are key qualitative differences between men and women [involved in the CJS] in the area of relationships which need to be made explicit, in particular … the high rates of domestic and other abuse many female offenders have endured which can be linked to their offending and, if ongoing, may mean some of their current relationships will not be conducive to their rehabilitation. (Farmer, 2019, p. 19)

Lord Farmer identified relationships as the most significant criminogenic need for women and expanded upon this by stating that women's relationships, and the issues that arise from them, can impact upon both women's offending *and* re-offending. As a consequence, the Farmer review suggested that in order for the CJS to improve the way it works with women who become involved in crime it needs to capture and consider a woman's history of abuse (Farmer, 2019).

Following the Farmer Review, the All Party Parliamentary Group (APPG) on Women in the Penal System published a briefing which once again drew attention to the prevalence of domestic abuse within the histories of women coming into contact with the CJS. The APPG referenced research undertaken by the Howard League which examined the backgrounds of women arrested by the police. Drawing upon arrest data collected from one police force over a 2-year period they found that in three quarters of women's arrests the women had already come into contact with the police but as *victims* of domestic or sexual violence (APPG on Women in the Penal System, 2020). As a consequence, the APPG concluded that: 'For too many women, contact with the police results in their criminalisation rather than a recognition that they might be victims of domestic abuse' (APPG on Women in the Penal System, 2020, p. 5).

As the introduction to this chapter has illustrated, in the UK there is a wealth of literature that testifies to a relationship between a woman's experience of domestic abuse and her involvement in crime. The majority of this literature is, however, policy-based and quantitative in nature, therefore providing little insight into the ways in which a woman's experience of domestic abuse may influence her pathway into crime. The remainder of the chapter will therefore summarise some of the existing literature which has attempted to explore the relationship in further detail.

---

[2]Lord Farmer was commissioned by the MOJ to undertake two separate reviews, one in 2017 (focussed on male prisoners) and another, referenced here, in 2019. Farmer's (2019) second review focused on women only and explored the impact of women's family and relational ties upon their offending and reoffending.

An Internationally Recognised Connection

Notably, evidence of women who come into contact with the CJS having disproportionately experienced abuse and trauma is not a discovery limited to the UK alone. Instead, the prevalence of domestic abuse and other forms of victimisation within the histories of women within the CJS has been documented worldwide including in America (Ferraro, 2006; Richie, 1996), Canada (Comack, 2000), and Australia (Segrave and Carlton, 2010). In 2014, the United Nations Office on Drugs and Crime (UNODC) provided an indication of the proportions of female prisoners who have histories of domestic abuse victimisation drawing on data from the UK, Europe, Canada, and the United States. The UNODC (2014) report indicated that in the United States 43 percent of women in prison reported a history of domestic or sexual abuse, in the UK 50 percent of women reported having experienced domestic abuse, and in Canada 83 percent of those surveyed at the Prison for Women reported being survivors of physical or sexual abuse.

Further evidence of the prevalence of domestic abuse victimisation experienced by women who come into contact with the CJS is available from Australia. In a recent report published by Australia's National Research Organisation for Women's Safety (ANROWS, 2020) they note how Australian studies consistently report that overwhelming numbers of women in custody have experienced abuse. The figure included in the report indicated that between 70 and 90 percent of women in prison have experienced physical, emotional, and/or sexual abuse which in the majority of cases is perpetrated by the women's spouses or partners (ANROWS, 2020). When examining the backgrounds of indigenous Aboriginal women or Torres Strait Islanders the figure increases to between 75 and 90 percent reporting experience of abuse (Australian Law Reform Commission, 2017).

Although the population of imprisoned women in Canada is relatively small, Canadian research provides a similar picture to that of Australia as a range of studies have identified high proportions of women in prison who have histories of abuse (see Tam and Derkzen, 2014). In 1990, the Task Force on Federally Sentenced Women published a report on the findings of interviews that had been conducted to better understand the backgrounds of women involved in crime. The Task Force reported that of the women that had been interviewed[3] 80 percent disclosed experience of abuse, 68 percent stated they had been physically abused, and 54 percent disclosed experience of sexual abuse (Task Force on Federally Sentenced Women, 1990). These findings led them to conclude that experience of abuse was extremely common within the backgrounds of many federally sentenced women. Furthermore, in their review of existing literature Tam and Derkzen (2014) identified a study by Barrett et al. (2010) which discovered that during their lifetimes just over three quarters of the female offender population had experienced physical abuse.

---

[3]The Task Force had undertaken interviews with 84 percent of all incarcerated women and 57 female offenders who were under mandatory supervision or on parole.

Crucially, there is international acknowledgement of the prevalence of histories of abuse within the demographic of women who come into conflict with the law. It is important to state that the vast majority of research that has been undertaken has concentrated on the female prisoner population, as opposed to women serving community-based sentences or those on parole. Unlike the mainly quantitative evidence and policy-based data which has been collected in the UK, internationally there has been a more extensive attempt to conceptualise and theoretically examine this link via qualitative examination of how domestic abuse may function as a driver to women's offending, some of which will be summarised below.

Victims of Domestic Abuse Murdering Their Abusers

Much of the early academic research which explored how a woman's experience of domestic abuse could influence her pathway into crime focussed upon cases where women had murdered their abusive partners (see Walker, 1984; Browne, 1987; Browne and Williams, 1989 and Jones, 1994). In 1984 in America the first large-scale piece of empirical research on this subject was published by Walker who established the concept of 'battered woman syndrome' (BWS). Walker's findings were based upon the experiences of 435 women who had been subjected to domestic abuse (although she employed the American term 'battering'). The term BWS, which Walker introduced, referred to a set of specific psychological and behavioural symptoms which resulted from prolonged and extensive exposure to abuse and which could contribute to a woman's motivation to murder her abusive partner and she identified stages that women might go through preceding the murder. Walker's study is now very outdated and has subsequently been the subject of widespread criticism which derives from the lack of evidence to support the concept of BWS. Criticism of Walker's work is also founded in the potential it has for presenting inaccurate stereotypes of victims' behaviour (Dutton, 2006).

Browne's (1987) study followed Walker's but employed a different approach, comparing the experiences of 42 women who had been charged with murdering or seriously injuring their abusive partners with the experiences of 205 women who had been subjected to domestic abuse but had not been involved in any crime against their abusers. Browne's (1987) study concluded that women who kill their abusers are an exception to the rule as victims of domestic abuse are not typically violent towards their partners, as they rarely initiate violence or respond to physical assaults perpetrated by the abuser. Browne (1987) also highlighted how victims of domestic abuse are far more likely to be killed by their abuser than the other way around. Browne's (1987) study concluded that the lack of options available to women when attempting to escape abusive relationships as well as the lack of effective legal interventions 'leaves many of these women alone with a danger from which they cannot escape' (Browne, 1987, p. 180). Browne's conclusions provide an important contribution to explaining how women's involvement in crime can be more broadly affected by their experiences of domestic abuse. Browne points to the absence of suitable interventions or protections for victims as impacting upon the choices they can make and the actions they can take if needing to exit an abusive relationship. Significantly, when comparing the differences between the groups of women that had committed violence against or killed their abusers and those who had not Browne identified that the former had been subjected to more frequent and serious abuse and abuse which targeted the women's children. Browne (1987) subsequently concluded that the victims of abuse had not taken violent action until the attacks they were subjected to became so severe that they were left with no other choice about how to protect themselves or their children.

The subject of women killing their abusive partners has recently been revisited, and this may be in part due to the Sally Challen case. In 2011, Sally Challen was convicted of murdering her abusive husband and was sentenced to life imprisonment, however, her sentence was subsequently challenged and she was freed after her conviction was overturned in 2020. The challenge to Sally's conviction was made due to her longstanding experience of coercive control and on account of this prosecutors accepted a manslaughter plea and accepted time served (Justice for Women, 2021; Bindel, 2018). During her appeal Sally Challen was supported by the Centre for Women's Justice (CWJ) and they recently published a report which examined the treatment of women who have killed their partners within the CJS. In their report the CWJ (2021) concluded that women murdering their partners do so as a last resort and as a consequence of a CJS that has failed to protect them from male violence.

The Relationship between Women and Their Male Co-Defendants

There is evidence to suggest that men can play a significant part in influencing women's involvement in crime (see, e.g., Jones, 2008; Gilfus, 1992, 2002; Welle and Falkin, 2000). Therefore, in order to better understand women's pathways into crime the influence that male co-defendants can have on their female counterparts is an area that has also been examined by academics (see Weare and Barlow, 2019; Welle and Falkin, 2000; Jones, 2008). Welle and Falkin (2000) conducted a study of 60 women who had taken part in crime with a male co-defendant and found that compared with women involved with 'non-romantic' co-defendants, the women involved with a 'romantic' co-defendant were more vulnerable to manipulation. The findings of their study also revealed that many of the women who had taken part in criminal activities with their romantic partners had been threatened or physically harmed by them and were often subjected to high levels of control. Welle and Falkin (2000) also noted that in many of the cases the male co-defendants had employed abuse to guarantee their partner's compliance with their offending. Welle and Falkin (2000, p. 46) introduced the term 'relationship policing' which they defined as the co-defendants' 'surveillance, control and punishment of their female partners'. They concluded that both 'relationship policing' and domestic abuse were integral to a process which trapped women into offending. Furthermore, they suggested that the 'un-policed' nature of the home effectively trapped women in their abusive relationships leaving them vulnerable to the coercion of their partners' circumstances which culminated in their pathways into crime.

Jones (2008) completed a similar study in England, interviewing 50 female prisoners about their experiences of crime with a co-defendant. His work revealed male co-defendants' widespread use of abusive techniques which they employed to ensure the women's compliance in their crimes. Jones (2008) identified how the male co-defendants had used physical violence, emotional abuse, manipulation and coercion as well as facilitating their partners' dependence on drugs, all of which had influenced the women's involvement in crime.

The findings of a more recent study, undertaken by Weare and Barlow (2019), identified how women's intimate relationships with their co-defendants can act as a 'catalyst' to their offending. In reference to the women who took part in their study, Weare and Barlow (2019) identified that the relationships between the women and their co-defendants were all characterised by the women's fear of their male partners. Weare and Barlow (2019) also noted that the men had employed coercive and controlling behaviours as well as perpetrated physical abuse against their female co-defendants. The study concluded that the women's pathways into crime had been heavily influenced by their relationship with their intimate partners and the abuse perpetrated by them.

How Women's Coping Mechanisms and Survival Strategies Can Affect Their Involvement in Crime

When attempting to understand how women's experiences of domestic abuse can influence their involvement in crime, key contributions have been made by both Chesney-Lind and Rodriguez (1983) and Gilfus (1992). Chesney-Lind and Rodriguez (1983, p. 62) suggest that the mechanisms that women employ to cope with or escape the abuse they are subjected to can result in 'a process of criminalisation unique to women'. In a later study, Chesney-Lind (1989, p. 11), referencing cases where women became involved in criminal activities to cope with or escape abusive relationships, labelled this: 'the criminalisation of ... survival strategies'.

In a later study Gilfus (1992) developed six, sometimes overlapping, pathways[4] which could lead women into crime, all of which resulted from their relationships with abusive men. One path of particular interest was path 6, which she described as 'enforcement violence'. 'Enforcement violence' is a process whereby domestic abuse victims are further victimised and trapped within abusive situations by mechanisms outside of the abuse itself, often a result of 'policies, laws and institutional practices' (Gilfus, 2002, p. 7) which can consequently label women's actions within an abusive relationship as criminal. One specific example provided by Gilfus highlighted how criminal justice agencies fail to treat women as victims when assessing their offence.

---

[4]The six pathways Gilfus (1992) developed were: abused girls who had run away; street workers (forced onto the streets as a result of the abuse they had experienced); women with substance abuse issues; women who had committed economic crime (often directly coerced by their abusers), women arrested for child abuse or women who had harmed their abuser, and women affected by 'enforcement violence'.

Here, Gilfus references a trend in social policy for prosecuting abused women for child abuse in cases where they are perceived to have 'failed to protect' their children. In these cases, the authorities disregard the abuse experienced by the women themselves, the lack of opportunity the women may have to intervene, and (most significantly) this policy is enforced even when the perpetrator of the abuse purposefully prevents the women from intervening in the abuse of her child. What is significant about this pathway is that it demonstrates how mechanisms outside of the abusive relationship itself can also impact upon how women's actions can be labelled as criminal.

Richie's (1996) work has also made a significant contribution to better understanding the relationship between domestic abuse and women's involvement in crime. Richie's work was based upon the experiences of African American women and she developed the concept of 'gender entrapment' which describes how women can become trapped into crime through a combination of factors including; gender, race, class oppression, and experience of abuse. Drawing upon the experiences of African American women who had been incarcerated Richie's work demonstrated '... how violence, threat of violence and other forms of coercion by their male partners led them to crime' (Richie, 1996, p. 15). Like Gilfus (1992) Richie also developed six pathways into crime which included: 'Women Held Hostage'; 'Projection and Association'; 'Sexual Exploitation'; 'Fighting Back'; 'Poverty' and 'Addiction' (Richie, 1996). Richie's study also identified how women could be criminalised as a result of the coping mechanisms they employed to manage their abuse or as a result of actions taken when fighting back against their abusers. It must be noted that Richie's work focussed upon a *combination* of factors leading to women's involvement in crime and therefore did not explicitly explain how domestic abuse *alone* influenced the women's pathways to crime.

Finally, Ferraro's (2006) later work represents one of the most notable attempts to examine how domestic abuse can influence women's pathways into crime. Drawing upon the accounts of 45 women who had experienced domestic abuse and been involved in crime, Ferraro identified multiple ways in which their domestic abuse victimisation had influenced their pathway into crime. Examples provided by Ferraro included women committing crime to placate their abuser, women offending due to fear of their abuser and the criminalisation of the women's survival strategies. Interestingly, Ferraro also suggested that a fracturing or distortion of victims' perceptions, which resulted from the domestic abuse they experienced, could lead to a rejection of moral codes or affect reasoning/decision-making, subsequently influencing women's pathways into crime. A limitation of Ferraro's study, however, was that all of the women involved in it had either committed an offence against their abusive partner or with them and, as a consequence, no wider exploration of the relationship between a woman's experience of domestic abuse and involvement in crime was possible.

Although what has been presented here is not an exhaustive analysis of all available literature in this area, what has been demonstrated is widespread evidence of the prevalence of domestic abuse victimisation in the histories of women who come into contact with the CJS. Moreover, the studies referenced in this chapter have also provided an insight into how a woman's experience of domestic abuse can influence her pathway into crime. With existing literature predominantly focussing on women in prison, what has been presented to date is how a woman's experience of domestic abuse can impact upon her involvement in rare and atypical forms of women's offending such as homicide, child abuse, and violence perpetrated by abuse victims against their abusive partners (to provide only a few examples). Consequently, what results from the existing literature is a partial and somewhat sensationalised picture which has often been accompanied by a narrow focus on women's involvement in crime where victims of domestic abuse offend with, against or on behalf of an abusive partner. Although these situations do occur, conclusions about how the relationship between a woman's experience of domestic abuse and her involvement in crime which depend only on existing research could be perceived as simplified, reductionist explanations. Consequently, there is a need for a broader and more qualitative investigation of how the relationship between a woman's experience of domestic abuse and her pathway into crime actually operates.

Chapter 4

Women's Pathways into Offending Manifesting as a By-product of Attempting to Cope With, Survive, Or Escape Domestic Abuse

The findings of the research outlined in this book were firmly embedded in the experiences, perceptions, accounts, and words of the women who generously donated their time to participate in the study. Established via the interviews with the women, the overarching theme which explained how domestic abuse could function as a driver to a woman's involvement in crime was *coping*. Elaborating upon the term coping, in this context it specifically refers to the actions women took, and the behaviours they enacted, in response to their domestic abuse victimisation. In particular, the women's accounts detailed how they coped with and responded to the distinct imbalance of power they were subjected to within their abusive relationships, something which was facilitated, created, or imposed by their abusers. In many cases, the women's coping options were significantly limited; first, by the domestic abuse they were subjected to, and second, their space for action was further restricted by other factors including poverty, lack of education, unemployment, and mental health issues (to provide just a few examples) which compounded their lack of options or opportunity for action. In some cases, however, these difficult circumstances developed as a consequence of the domestic abuse the women were subjected to or in fact had been introduced by the perpetrators of abuse.

Therefore, the women's coping options were often distinctly limited both inside and outside of their abusive relationships. Ultimately, however, the women's discourses illustrated how the crimes they had committed often manifested as a *by-product* of their experiences of domestic abuse, or more explicitly their attempts to cope with the domestic abuse they were being subjected to.

The women's involvement in crime, therefore, manifested as a *by-product* of the actions they took to cope with domestic abuse which included:

Gendered Justice? How Women's Attempts to Cope With, Survive, or Escape Domestic Abuse Can Drive Them into Crime, 25–28
Copyright © 2022 by Jo Roberts
Published under exclusive licence by Emerald Publishing Limited
doi:10.1108/978-1-80262-069-620221005

- Their responses to the abuse they were subjected to.
- Their attempts to survive their abuse (their survival strategies).
- Their attempts to resist abuse.
- Their attempts to escape their abusive relationship (whether that be temporarily, permanently, figuratively, or literally).
- Their exit from an abusive relationship or situation.

The Wide-reaching Impact of Domestic Abuse Victimisation

Importantly, the findings of this research suggest that women's criminal offences can occur in a much broader context than has previously been acknowledged. Rather than women simply offending against an abuse perpetrator, with an abuse perpetrator or being forced or coerced by an abuse perpetrator to commit a crime, instead crimes can be committed by women who have been subjected to domestic abuse:

- Without the abuser present.
- After they have exited an abusive relationship or situation.
- Many years after the relationship/abuse has ended.

In all of these cases, however, the women's behaviour and actions can still be attributed, in some way, to their experiences of domestic abuse. Therefore, this research demonstrated both the immediate and longitudinal impact that domestic abuse victimisation can have upon a woman's behaviour and actions.

The different ways in which women's involvement in crime can be connected to their experience of domestic abuse is illustrated by the figure below, where coping was identified as the overarching theme and underneath further subthemes are provided accompanied by some illustrative examples (see Fig. 4.1).

The study described in this book differentiates itself from existing research which has largely considered the experiences of women in prison by focussing on the lives and experiences of women serving community-based sentences. As a result, the study was able to explore a much broader range of crimes more reflective of the gendered patterns of offending including theft, drink-driving, benefit fraud, and drugs offences (to provide just some examples). Unlike the already existing studies, this research also paid particular attention to women's immediate and *longer-term* responses to their domestic abuse victimisation and examined both the *direct* and *indirect* ways in which such experiences could bring them into contact with the CJS. As a consequence of focussing on women serving community-based sentences and employing a wider, longer-term approach, this study established that the ways in which women's experiences of domestic abuse can be connected to their pathways into crime are much broader than has previously been considered.

Although the study did find evidence to corroborate theories generated by already established studies, the findings of this research did, however, determine a

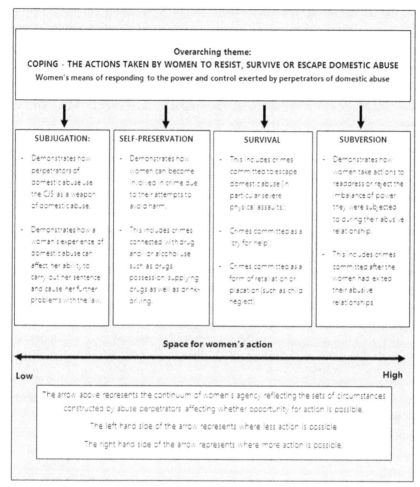

Fig. 4.1.   Themes Arising from the Interviews with the Women Where Coping
Is Identified as the Overarching Theme.

need to adopt a wider and more longitudinal focus in order to adequately explain
how a woman's experience of domestic abuse can influence her pathway into crime.

Coping with and Responding to Domestic Abuse

Prior to presenting the women's narratives which describe a range of ways in
which the coping mechanisms they employed when responding to the domestic
abuse they were subjected to brought them into conflict with the law it is important to discuss the term 'coping'. The particular definition referenced in this
book is based upon that used by Kelly (1988). In Kelly's study of the techniques

women employ to survive sexual and other forms of male violence she describes coping as: 'the actions taken to avoid or control distress [where] women's coping responses are active, constructive adaptations to experiences of abuse' (Kelly, 1988, p. 160). This particular definition was employed for this study as a result of the feminist approach taken which recognises all women's responses to their experiences of abuse, whether outwardly perceived as passive or active, comprise a form of action taken by the women in response to their victimisation. Not only does this definition adhere to the feminist approach of the research, it also aligns closely with the symbolic interactionist perspective,[1] which was employed as it recognises the individual and subjective nature of each woman's abusive relationship as well as the types and tactics of abuse used by the abuse perpetrators. As Kelly (1988, p. 160) elaborates:

> The responses of any particular woman will depend on how she defines her experience, the context within which it occurs and the resources which are available to her at the time [of the violence/ abuse] and subsequently.

Although the approach taken in this research attests to the agency involved in the women's actions and responses, it also recognises that not all responses or means of coping will be recognised as agentic nor will they all have positive outcomes. Consequently, Kelly (1988) notes that the effectiveness of the women's strategies may vary, both in the short or long term, and in addition the coping mechanisms that women employ may involve some 'costs' to them. For women who are subjected to domestic abuse, or coercive control, Stark (2007, p. 216) argues that agency and victimisation co-exist simultaneously and women attempt to exercise:

> [...] 'control in the context of no control'. This seeming paradox is actualised in both the literal assertion of subjectivity in abusive relationships through open resistance, refusal, and the adaptation of safety and survival plans and when women nest their subjectivity in behaviours, control strategies or personhood while conveying seeming compliance to the perpetrator.

Therefore, the restrictions on women's behaviour enforced and conditioned by the domestic abuse perpetrated against them do not completely prevent women from taking some form of action, whether appearing passive or acquiescing to the abuse perpetrator. The actions taken by the women to cope with their experiences of domestic abuse, and how such actions influenced their involvement in crime, will now be explored through the women's accounts.

---

[1] For further information about symbolic interactionism and the theoretical foundations of the study see Appendix A.

Chapter 5

May and Robin: How Women's Involvement in Crime Can Manifest as a By-product of Coping with or Surviving Domestic Abuse

May was 48 when she was interviewed for the study and she had two adult children aged 28 and 24. She had left school at an early age and didn't have any formal qualifications but had been working with life-long learning to gain some practical qualifications whilst she was serving her sentence. May had been married twice (the first time at the age of 18), divorced twice and subsequently had other relationships with men and May described all of her relationships as abusive. May's probation file identified that she had experienced significant problems in previous relationships and notes from her OASys assessment stated that she was 'vulnerable to the influence of abusive males'. Further information from her file linked her offending behaviour to issues in her relationships as well as her alcohol use. May had a long history of offending and many of her convictions were drink related (she had been convicted of three offences related to drunkenness).

May had been subjected to both physical and emotional abuse by multiple partners and she described what her most recent relationship had been like:

> We were just drinking partners, but then when I fell for him …
> I told him I loved him, treated me like dirt ever since, just treated
> me like a lump of dirt ever since, started hitting me, then he come
> back down the following day say he was sorry and I was the fool
> that took him back and the hitting went worse, the hitting did go
> worse and then I hit the drink again, I hid behind the bottle.

May was in a relationship with this man for 4 years and she detailed how the abuse became worse as the relationship continued, with him subjecting her to sexual abuse and a severe physical attack after which she ended the relationship:

Gendered Justice? How Women's Attempts to Cope With, Survive,
or Escape Domestic Abuse Can Drive Them into Crime, 29–39
Copyright © 2022 by Jo Roberts
Published under exclusive licence by Emerald Publishing Limited
doi:10.1108/978-1-80262-069-620221006

> In the last 12 months, [he was really] controlling then, when he wanted sex, I'd have to, I'd have to give him sex. Perhaps I wouldn't feel like it, [but] just for the peace, do you know what I mean? … Well the relationship ended when the police went and found me on my laminated flooring full of blood … he cut me in the temple of the head. I had 2 black eyes, bleeding nose, and he was banging my head against the laminated floor and that's all I can remember ….

May explained that she had turned to alcohol as a way to cope with the abuse she had experienced:

> I hid, I hid behind that bottle see, to get rid of the black eyes, to get rid of the hurt, you know, he never said he loved me once and yet I put up with him for four years. The hitting, he'd say sorry, I'd take him back, the hitting would get worse then, 'you love being hit', he used to say to me.

There was a high prevalence of substance use within the histories of the women who were involved in the study as 21 of the 25 women interviewed disclosed using alcohol or drugs, or in some cases both.[1] Like the situation May describes above, many of the women explained that their substance use was symptomatic of their experience of abuse as they employed alcohol or drugs as a means of managing, coping, escaping, or 'blocking out' their abuse. In many cases their substance use was described as a means of numbing either the emotional or physical pain they were subjected to by their abusers. Importantly the women's interviews revealed that alcohol or drugs could be used as a coping mechanism both during or after the women's abusive relationships, and in some cases the alcohol or drug use continued long after the relationship had ended. This use of drugs or alcohol by the women was labelled as a form of 'self-preservation' as this is defined by their attempts to avoid harm.

Women resorting to the use of substances as a means of coping with abuse is something that has also been recognised by Women's Aid (2011). In Women's Aid's (2011) guidance for working with female offenders who have experienced domestic abuse they referenced a study by Humphries and Regan (2005) which identified that for nearly two-thirds of the women involved in their study coping with domestic abuse provided the explanation for their problematic substance use. Furthermore, evidence also indicates that when compared to the wider female population women who have been subjected to domestic abuse are fifteen times more likely to misuse alcohol and nine times more likely to misuse drugs (Stark and Flitcraft, 1996).

When asked if she felt her experiences of domestic abuse had contributed to her offences (many of which were for drunk and disorderly), May responded:

---

[1]The women's substance use was either recorded on their Probation file from their OASys assessment or was disclosed by the women in their interviews.

It's ... a lot to do with domestic abuse, the black eyes ... hid behind the bottle. It's all to do with ... every man I've had they have put me down into a gutter and I mean literally in the gutter, you know, I'll feel like, I was trying to climb that ladder and I was sliding back down it like a piece of slime.

May's recollection of her experiences suggest that she employed alcohol as a means of figuratively escaping the domestic abuse she was subjected to within multiple relationships and although she had tried to escape, as she described it she kept 'sliding back down'. May's alcohol dependence, her method of coping with years of abuse, combined with the total erosion of her self-esteem facilitated by the abuse, subsequently led to her becoming an alcoholic and it was under the influence of alcohol that the vast majority of May's crimes had been committed.[2] The relationship between May's alcohol use and her involvement in crime is demonstrated by the offences May had been convicted of as she had three separate convictions for drunk and disorderly as well as convictions for assault which she said had been committed under the influence of alcohol.

Although Summer was convicted of an offence that was unrelated to alcohol or substance use, like May, she disclosed how she used alcohol as a means of coping with the abuse she experienced:

[During] the abuse and all that, I was heavy on the drink, that's how I'd deal with my problems ... we'd go for the litre ones then so I used to drink at least 3 and a half litres a day, daily, never thought I was like drunk ... you know like people go for a cup of tea, that's how I used to go for the vodka and it wasn't necked down it was, do you know what I mean, any stress it was, it was I needed a vodka.

Both May and Summer's cases demonstrate that some women adopt avoidant coping strategies, such as consuming alcohol, as a form of self-medication where they may be unable to directly address, or escape, the abuse they are being subjected to. This behaviour is not uncommon for survivors of domestic abuse as Kaysen et al. (2007, p. 1280) found in their study examining domestic abuse victims' motivations for alcohol use:

[...] self-medication is a viable explanatory model in those with more severe trauma symptoms who believe that alcohol is a useful way to cope [but they] are at greater risk for heavy alcohol use and maladaptive coping.

---

[2]It is important to state that of course not all women who use substances as a means of escaping or coping with the domestic abuse they are being/were subjected to become involved in crime due to being under the influence of alcohol or drugs. This was, however, the explanation provided by May for her pathway into offending.

In addition the destruction of a woman's self-esteem, which has been identified by Kirkwood (1993) as a key dynamic of domestic abuse, may also be a contributory factor to women's pathways into crime. The abuse women are subjected to can shatter their feelings of self-worth and self-esteem leading them to believe there is no future for them and as a consequence women can sometimes have little concern about their own opportunities or well-being. As May expresses, when she was in her last abusive relationship, she felt she had no future: 'I got a future now, which I thought I never did have, there was no light at the end of that tunnel for me'. Studies have found that for some women involvement in crime is of very little consideration to them when compared with their attempts to simply cope with the abuse they are being subjected to (see Ferraro, 2006 and Richie, 1996). Therefore, for May, her involvement in crime can be seen to have manifested as a by-product of the coping mechanisms she employed to manage her multiple experiences of abuse.

It was not only May who spoke about turning to substances as a means of coping with the abuse she had experienced. Robin was 36 and had become pregnant with her only child at the age of 15 and subsequently left school without any qualifications. Her child was taken into care when he was 2 and Robin was in the process of re-establishing a relationship with him at the time she took part in the study. At the time of her interview, she was serving a sentence for possession of class A drugs (heroin) and she had a history of drugs-related offences including distribution.

During her interview Robin spoke about one of her partners who had subjected her to severe physical violence as well as multiple other forms of abuse. She had been in a relationship with this man for 4 years and felt that the abuse she had experienced was linked to her offending. Robin described some of the severe violent incidents that had taken place during the time she was with her ex-partner:

> I remember one incident where he, I had my hand out on the table, as you can see on my finger here [shows interviewer finger with part missing] and he chopped my finger off with a machete … he had pitbulls and staffs, he set the pitbull on me, I mean, I still got bite marks all up here, I mean, [probation officer] was looking at them, she says it's awful. You know, meat prongs he'd go for me with ….

Not only had Robin's partner subjected her to violence he had also been verbally abusive to her and controlled her movements, as she describes:

> 'oi, slut' – this is the way he used to talk to me – 'get fucking dressed, it's 2 o'clock and I gotta collect my giro at 3 o'clock'. I said, 'give me 2 minutes', now he took this as me being, answering back, 'give me 2 minutes', I said, you know, give me half a chance and I'll get dressed. So I've got dressed, come downstairs, next thing, dirty mop bucket, you know the metal mop buckets, the old-fashioned wooden thick handles, he threw the dirty mop water all over me and snapped the very thick pole it was, I'd call

it, snapped it over my back 4 times, into 4 separate pieces …. Next thing, taxi beeps outside, 'now fucking get in the car', he said to me, 'you're coming with me to collect the giro', 'cause he knew I would have gone, I'd've run and you know … I suffered many beatings, from beatings daily … I mean I've got a perforated ear-drum … I'm shouting because my hearing's bad because of it and you know, I have many scars where he's stabbed me, he's stabbed me here, chopped my finger off.

Robin described how she had turned to drugs as a means of self-medication, as a way to figuratively escape the abuse, she was being subjected to:

It is self-medicating the brain. It's like you go to the doctor, the doctor gives you a Valium, to keep you calm, do you understand? But to me, heroin, at that time, was my drug. I was self-medicating to just shut off from the world.

Although Robin had used drugs prior to her abusive relationship, she explained how she had started using stronger drugs after a particular incident had taken place:

I just turned to heroin from there just to switch off from what was going on and it turned from that to … just got out of control, so I started selling heroin myself just 3 years ago and ended up doing a 3-year prison sentence.

Robin explained that she had turned to heroin after her abuser murdered one of her male friends in front of her; devastating actions which could be perceived to be an attempt by her abusive partner to instil fear and exert absolute control over Robin. Robin described the murder:

[my abusive ex-partner] had [my friend] cornered in the corner and I'll never forget it, within my eye view of the kitchen door … he's holding a big chef's carving knife in his hand, and as I've gone "don't!" and I didn't even get to "d" you know when you go "d…", he's plunged it into him … severed his femoral artery, fractured his pelvis bone, there was no way he gonna survive that, no way … that whole kitchen was full of clotted blood, lumps of liver, what looked like liver, but it was congealed blood from his femoral artery … I could see he was going and I got 999 on the phone … I, I knew he was dying, I could see it, I could see it and I could feel it, I can't explain it to you. So all I remember was [ex-partner] going out the front door, going into the alleyway.

Not only did Robin's partner commit the murder in front of her, as an extension of the abuse he had already inflicted upon her he also claimed that Robin had actually committed the crime:

[ex-partner] was telling the police that I'd done it [the murder].
Yeah, so not only did he physically torture me, he mentally tortured me and my family for 14 months and he was gonna go all
the way except for the day in trial he accepted a manslaughter plea
and he had 4 and a half years for that.

As stated earlier, it was after the murder that Robin started to use heroin and
she explained how this had helped her cope with her memories of the murder:

I liked how it [heroin] made me forget … it's like three levels when
you're using heroin. You're beginning, oh, this is good, this is
great, this is making me feel so comfortable and relaxed, and I can
forget everything. You've got the second stage which you think,
right, where's my next fix coming tomorrow. You're thinking a day
ahead. Then it gets to the point where you think I have to go out
and either sell my body, commit a crime or, sell some drugs to get
my next fix.

As this interview extract demonstrates, Robin coped with her highly traumatic
experiences of abuse and the murder her abusive partner committed in her presence by using heroin, an extremely addictive drug, and, as a consequence, this led
to her involvement in crime as a means of her being able to continue supplying
herself with heroin. Robin explained how she perceived her experiences of abuse
to be linked to her involvement in crime:

that's what it did for me, the abuse over the years led me to take
drugs to forget things. And in the end, I hit such a low point in
my life, you know, I ended up selling [drugs]. It seemed the easi-
est thing to do. I knew in the end I was gonna to get caught, but
maybe deep down, part of me wanted to get caught.

Robin was asked directly if she felt that the domestic abuse she was subjected
to had influenced her pathway into crime and she responded:

[…] if I hadn't had so much trauma in my life I wouldn't have
turned to drugs, I wouldn't have turned to selling drugs, hence not
going to jail, you know. And now I haven't got all that abuse in
my life I don't feel the need to go and buy drugs or sell drugs, so
it has yeah.

Robin's case provides an example where a clear connection can be drawn
between her extremely traumatic experiences of domestic abuse and her drug use,
which in itself is a crime, followed by the escalation of her drug use after a further
traumatic event, which then led to her further offending to fund her heroin use.
Her situation therefore provides an example of Moloney et al.'s (2009) theory
that women's involvement in crime can start with their self-medication or use of

substances as a means of coping with unresolved trauma which can subsequently lead to women's involvement in crime via drug-related offences. It is important at this stage to note that for many women their use of drugs or alcohol is introduced, or actively encouraged, by perpetrators of abuse, something which has been extensively commented on in domestic abuse literature (see Women's Aid, 2011; Jones, 2008; Ferraro, 2006; Moe, 2004 and Inciardi et al., 1993). This can be perceived to be a tactic employed by perpetrators of domestic abuse as a mechanism of control often used to facilitate the victim's further dependency on the perpetrator (particularly if they are the provider of the drugs to their partner).

Maloney et al. (2009) previously identified that women's drug use, employed as a response to experiencing trauma, can also contribute to their pathways into crime indirectly via their attempts to obtain money for drugs using methods such as prostitution and theft. They also noted how women's substance use could affect a woman's involvement in crime as a result of anti-social behaviour enacted when under the influence of substances, circumstances which are illustrated by May's case.

One of the probation staff interviewed mentioned the prevalence of substance use by women in contact with the CJS:

> usually drugs and alcohol use seems to be higher than average for female offenders, [they] seem to have high either drug or alcohol use, and I don't know if that's a coping strategy .... (Probation staff member 3)

In their recent publication the PRT (2017a) reported that many of the women in prison they had spoken to had disclosed that they had turned to substance use as a means of coping with abuse and on entry to prison women are far more likely to ask for help with drug use than men. These findings support Moe's (2004) work on women, crime, and drugs which identified that drug use functioned as an alternative method of surviving domestic abuse via the numbing of emotions. Moe (2004) also demonstrated how a woman's drug use, employed as a means of coping with domestic abuse, could then lead to women's further problems within the CJS as a result of engaging in other illegal activities to fund drug use such as theft and prostitution.

Within this study multiple probation staff also provided examples that further substantiate Moe's (2004) claims as they perceived that the coping mechanisms that some women employ to manage the abuse they are being subjected to can be very much related to the offences they are convicted of, as this probation staff member notes:

> The alcohol use or, and/or drug misuse will become a coping mechanism for where there are things going on that are unmanageable for the person ... in terms of domestic violence ... even if [women are] not into drug misuse and offending generally, they will quite often use alcohol as a coping mechanism to hide away from some of the issues and then that can lead into offending then

whether it be in terms of violent or aggressive or disruptive behaviour, or whether it be the acquisitive side of offending, in terms of the need to get money for substances, and there can be issues of child neglect and things that come around that side because they're, it's partly to do with the issues they're suffering and partly to do with their coping mechanisms which then make the situation worse for the children involved and so they may often be offenders on that side of things. (Probation staff member 15)

As this probation staff member illustrates, women's pathways into crime can be heavily influenced by the coping mechanisms they employ to deal with domestic abuse or, in other words, the women's involvement in crime manifests as a by-product of the domestic abuse they are currently experiencing or have experienced. This theory also suggests that the women's involvement in crime is not deliberate but instead takes place as a by-product of different forms of self-preservation, self-medication or indeed just simply attempting to survive being subjected to domestic abuse.

The women's involvement in crime can also manifest in a longer-term context as a result of their actions to sustain long-term drug habits, for example. In specific reference to cases of child neglect probation staff member 15 expands upon how a woman's coping mechanisms can have a direct impact upon such offences:

I think in terms of neglect, so in terms of the woman having so many issues of her own going on, linked with abuse, linked with substance misuse, that actually they end up not then caring for the children in the way that they should because they feel unable to... and that could take a variety of forms ... there might just be more pure neglect where they're just not looking after their [child/ren's] emotional needs or they're not feeding them, dressing them appropriately or whatever because they're just so chaotic themselves that they're not providing that basic care for children. (Probation staff member 15)

Significantly, multiple probation staff interviews established that women can be convicted of child neglect offences which result from the coping mechanisms they had employed to manage being subjected to domestic abuse. Such cases often reflected the centrality of the women's experience of abuse within their lives where their survival had to take precedence over everything else, leading to the woman's diminished ability to care for her children, as this staff member noted:

There'd be other [cases] where, as a by-product of domestic abuse then there's allegations of child neglect or failing to protect your child, or the child not going to school, because surviving that relationship becomes paramount ... the cases that come up regularly at the Multi-Agency Risk Assessment Conference (MARAC) are those people where the domestic abuse is such that they, surviving that relationship means that they're not able to focus and attend to the children…because [of] the preoccupation of surviving the relationship the children have much less attention. (Probation staff member 9)

Another probation staff member elaborated further upon the relationship between a woman's coping mechanisms and her involvement in crime:

[One of the women I am supervising, her] offending is to do with her children, neglect of her children, not sending them to school and that's because, so it's an indirect link, her drug and alcohol use has gone up, as a result of her [abusive] partner, so she's, when she's tried to get hold of it but she's not able to cope with her children. (Probation staff member 3)

In specific reference to women's relationships with their children, as the above quotations have suggested, situations can also occur where the behaviour of perpetrators of domestic abuse can force women to have to choose between acting to protect themselves or cope with the domestic abuse they are experiencing and acting to protect/care for their children where the latter can have fatal consequences for the women. In cases where women are convicted of child abuse or neglect this can often result from the mother's inability to care for or protect her children whilst she is being subjected to domestic abuse and circumstances such as these have been labelled by Stark (2007, p. 253) as 'the battered mother's dilemma'. The psychology of circumstances such as these can be interpreted using the term 'cognitive dissonance' (see Festinger, 1957) which refers to women being placed in a position of tension and discomfort (or indeed trauma) which are facilitated by holding beliefs that strongly conflict with one another. An example of this cognitive dissonance would include a woman behaving in a particular way, such as using drugs as a means of coping with being subjected to domestic abuse, where the woman understands that these actions of her own self-preservation may either directly or indirectly cause harm to her children (e.g., resulting in a reduced ability for her to care for her children). To provide another example, a mother, when unable to intervene in the abuse of her children being perpetrated by her partner would of course comprehend that what she is being instructed to do (take no action) is wrong. Her actions would be accompanied by experiencing conflict between her actions and her beliefs (and she would likely experience significant discomfort in not intervening); however, she would be compelled into obeying her abuser as a result of her understanding of what could happen to her should she not comply with her abuser's request (which could result in her death). Therefore, abuse perpetrators can cultivate circumstances which force women's compliance (or indeed complete restriction upon any choice of how to behave) where there is a significant discrepancy between the actions taken by the abuse victim and the actual beliefs held by them (see Malim and Birch, 1998). Stark further elaborates upon such dilemmas describing how the abuse perpetrator:

[...] repeatedly forces a victimized caretaker to choose between taking some action she believes is wrong (such as physically disciplining her child in inappropriate ways), being hurt herself, or standing by whilst he hurts the child. Confronted with these dilemmas, victims attempt to preserve their rationality and humanity by selecting the least dangerous option .... (Stark, 2007, p. 253).

Circumstances such as those outlined above, established by abuse perpetrators, create situations in which victims of domestic abuse are forced to make choices about how to act when in reality there is no real choice, they are simply forced to 'choose' the least dangerous option for them. Consequently, the 'battered woman's dilemma' can lead to women's involvement in crime through perceived child neglect or abuse where the woman is unable to protect or care for her children, as this probation staff member states:

I think from the child neglect point of view, in my experience of that, where a woman has just been struggling to cope because her main focus has been on keeping her [abusive] relationship at a level where things are gonna tick and nothing's gonna go wrong, so the priority's been on the partner, the money has gone on the partner's drug misuse, for example, that's then left the family unable to kind of survive but, again, through the fear and control, whilst the woman was able to recognise that her children weren't having adequate care she felt she didn't have the power to stand up to her partner and then we go down the route of we've got a situation of neglect 'cause things have really escalated out of control. (Probation staff member 11)

In cases of perceived child neglect where mothers are victims of domestic abuse there can be a lack of understanding from criminal justice agencies regarding the constraints the mothers are forced to act under (or are powerless to act under) which can lead to further punishment of the victim (or her criminalisation). As Stark (2007, p. 253) contends 'ignorance of the constraints under which a caretaker is responding often leads agencies to mistakenly hold her culpable and respond punitively, thereby aggravating rather than relieving the dilemma'. Not only does a punitive/criminal justice enforced response fail to recognise the often distinctly limited range of actions available to victims of domestic abuse, but contained within this treatment of mothers are biases associated with socially constructed gender roles (Stark, 1999). When the gendered expectations accompanying motherhood, where women are viewed as the primary caregivers and 'protectors' of their children, are not met this can subsequently lead to punitive enforcement by the CJS, reflecting societal perceptions that the woman has failed in her role as mother (Stark, 1999). The relationship between a woman's experience of domestic abuse, the methods employed to cope with the abuse, and the impact this can have on the woman's children suggest that a more comprehensive understanding of the holistic effects of domestic abuse upon a woman's actions and behaviours should be held by criminal justice agencies. Such considerations are supported by the London Safeguarding Children Board (2008) who recognise that a mother's experience of domestic abuse may diminish her capacity to be able to protect or adequately take care of her children, circumstances which reflect the woman's preoccupation with her own survival within her abusive relationship. Therefore, when attempting to understand a woman's behaviour, criminal justice agencies and practitioners must acknowledge the: '… restraints on the mother's liberty as the key element in battering, [and therefore recognise that] accountability for harming the children falls squarely with the batterer' (Stark, 1999, p. 106).

A Note on Coping and Agency

Both May and Robin's recollections of their experiences clearly evidence how women who have experienced domestic abuse can turn to different forms of substances as a means of coping with their experiences and, as a consequence, how this can lead to their involvement in crime. In reference to the cases discussed above it may be argued that the circumstances created by domestic abuse perpetrators can restrict women's abilities to respond to, or opportunities to exit, abusive relationships only allowing them figurative forms of escape. Forms of coping, such as the use of drugs or alcohol, are often viewed as passive or inactive forms of coping; however, it is important to recognise the limited contexts and opportunities in which women, who are subjected to domestic abuse, may have for any form of action or indeed escape. Consequently, Wilcox (2006, p. 31) insists that such acts should not be misinterpreted as passive but instead should be acknowledged as '… agentic acts of self-preservation (even though they may appear to be self-destructive)'. At this stage it is therefore vital to discuss the levels of agency involved in women's responses to domestic abuse emphasising that women are not simply passive recipients of abuse (see Stark, 2007 and Kirkwood, 1993). Instead, there is a myriad of evidence that women actively adopt and develop methods to survive their experiences and these actions involve both agency and process, which can be employed during, or after, their experience of victimisation (see Stark, 2007; Wilcox, 2006; Lempert, 1996; Kirkwood, 1993 and Kelly, 1988). Wilcox (2006) in particular comments upon how the actions taken by victims of domestic abuse may be perceived as passive by outside observers, but she argues that any coping mechanism employed is agentic with passivity itself functioning as a means of self-preservation. Lempert (1996, p. 281, emphasis added) supports Wilcox's assertion 'From the viewpoint of the actor, passive resistance was a strategic mode of *action* undertaken in preservation of self'. Lempert's (1996, p. 270) work also further supports the agentic nature of women's coping mechanisms as she asserts 'Abused women are active, although not co-acting equals, in the interactions with their partners; in the development of their own strategies to halt, change, and/or cope with the violence'. Despite the agency involved in the strategies women employ to cope with their experiences of domestic abuse and trauma it must also be recognised that such actions may not always have positive outcome for the actor (Wilcox, 2006; Lempert, 1996).

Chapter 6

Charlie, Donna, Skye and Ellie: Offending to Escape or Survive Abuse

> It was either my boyfriend was going to beat me to death or
> I was going to commit crime to go to prison, where I am going
> to be safe…I'm actually gonna be able to eat, I'm not going to be
> pimped out for money, for drugs I don't want to take anymore…
> when that steel [prison] door shuts it's the only time I can actually
> breathe properly. (Charlie)

For victims of domestic abuse their lives can be characterised by on-going attempts to survive the abuse they are subjected to and in these cases the women's actions can be driven by their attempts to prevent, avoid, or escape abuse. For some women, particularly those subjected to high levels of control by their abusive partner, their options of escape can be severely limited. Subsequently, as the quotation above illustrates, some women commit crime with the intention of being sent to prison, as this can, if they're successful, provide a sole opportunity of escape, or in some cases, respite from their victimisation. Therefore, for a number of the women involved in the study it was the actions they took to escape, minimise, or avoid abuse (particularly severe physical attacks) that brought them into contact with the CJS. The accounts included in this chapter provide examples of the actions that women took whilst still involved with an abusive partner and therefore can be categorised as immediate, rather than long-term, responses to their victimisation and consequently all such reactions were labelled as women's 'survival' attempts.

Charlie was 28 when she was interviewed for the study and her most recent offence was a breach of her licence conditions after she had been released from prison. Charlie had a long history of involvement in crime and had been involved with the CJS on multiple occasions, mainly for theft-related offences. Her life had been blighted by a long history of abuse which she had been subjected to both as a child and as an adult. During her short life all of Charlie's relationships, both inside and outside of her family, had been characterised by severe abuse. She recalls some of the abuse she was subjected to:

Gendered Justice? How Women's Attempts to Cope With, Survive,
or Escape Domestic Abuse Can Drive Them into Crime, 41–50
Copyright © 2022 by Jo Roberts
Published under exclusive licence by Emerald Publishing Limited
doi:10.1108/978-1-80262-069-620221007

> I've been tortured, I've had my hair set on fire … I've had real bad things happen to me, I've had my jaw broken, I've had my nose bust 3 times … he broke my nose, he put me on a 3 year waiting list for hospital to have my nose fixed. I had it done, they had to re-break my nose to fix my nose, so I came out of the hospital with 2 massive black eyes, which I didn't go in with, and then about 2 weeks later, then when I was healed, he smashed me in the nose again and told me he'd done it on purpose for the 3 years … and sexual abuse was me being prostituted out.

Charlie's description of the type of abuse she was subjected to, in particular the violent physical assaults, provide clear context to the levels of fear she experienced within her relationship and as the introductory quotation highlights, the actions that led to her being recalled to prison were driven by her fear of her abuser. Charlie's fear of, combined with her limited options of escape from, her controlling and violent partner motivated her to take actions which she knew would facilitate her return to prison, one of the only places she felt safe. She elaborates on the actions she took in response to being severely physically abused, driven by her desire to survive:

> I've … gone out, after my boyfriend's beaten me up, I've walked down the street and I've smashed every, like, seven car windows … just to get locked up … I've walked into shops and picked things up in front of security guards and walked out … I've done that about 30 times…to go to prison, go back to prison. Safer … it's the only place I am safe like, behind that steel door. (Charlie)

As Charlie states the only place she felt safe was in prison, where she was physically removed from her partner: 'every relationship I've been in I know that I'm better off when that steel door shuts, I can just go "pheww" [and relax]'.

When asked what had caused her to take actions which from an outside perspective may appear to be extreme, Charlie explained it was her 'complete and utter fear of dying' that led to her desperate actions. Notably, Charlie's fear of being murdered by her abuser is not unusual for victims of domestic abuse and is legitimised by the statistics available regarding the numbers of women who have been killed by their current or former partners. Karen Ingala Smith (2021) recorded the numbers of women killed by men in the years between 2009 and 2018 in the UK for the 10-year *Femicide Census* and during this time 1,425 women were murdered. During these 10 years the number of women killed each year did not fluctuate significantly; with 124 being the lowest number of women murdered in one year (in 2016) and the highest being 168 (in 2010). Subsequently the data collected for the census demonstrate that, on average, a woman is killed by a man every 3 days in the UK. In specific reference to the impact of domestic abuse, during this 10-year period in 62 percent of the cases where women were murdered, they were killed by their current or former partner (Smith, 2021). Furthermore, in 59 percent of the 1,042 femicides where the murder was committed by a partner, ex-partner or male family member there was a known history of abuse and in one-third of these cases the perpetrator had previously been reported to the police (Smith, 2021). In addition, Kelly's (1988) work *Surviving Sexual Violence*, which examined women's responses to a range of forms of sexual violence and abuse, also provides context and validation for Charlie's perspective as Kelly identified that fear of death is a common response to victims' experiences of abuse, or physical assaults. Kelly also emphasised that many women do not survive their experience of sexual assault and this is also true of domestic abuse (as highlighted by the *Femicide Census*) a context which further legitimises Charlie's perspective.

During the interviews Charlie was not the only woman who spoke about using the CJS as a route of escape from her abuser. Donna described how she deliberately tried to get arrested in the hope that she would be detained overnight in order to avoid a physical assault from her partner. Donna, aged 30, had been involved in two abusive relationships which had lasted nearly 14 years. Donna described how her most recent partner was known to the police and had a reputation for being violent '[he was] known for knives … he's known to the police for weapons and street robberies'. During her interview Donna described some of the severe physical abuse her partner had subjected her to during their relationship: 'he gripped me by my hair, dragged me off the chair and he was stamping on me, cracked all my ribs, he would not get off me'. Donna's abusive partner was not only physically abusive, he also used threats and weapons to frighten and control her. She recalled an incident which took place after she went on a night out with her sister describing what transpired when she returned home:

> he's sat there with a hammer in his hand, smashed my lamp, [poured] paint all over my brand new carpet which I'd just paid for and all over my bed … [and] every single item of my clothing … even my underwear and he'd put it all on my bed and tipped all paint, gloss, all over them, so I couldn't go out again and all down my brand new stair carpet and he sat there, smashed my brand new lamp I just paid £100 for. With a hammer in his hand, all paint down his jeans, he said 'I'm gonna kill you'.

Donna's various accounts of her partner's abusive behaviours provide a clear context to the actions she took which led to her arrest for assaulting a police officer. In Donna's case it was her desire to escape an expected physical assault that led to the actions she took, which she hoped she would be arrested and detained for. Donna explained:

> With [my abusive ex-partner], it was getting really serious, the violence …. He was hitting me. [I] wasn't allowed out or he'd want to come out and if we'd go out, we'd go together. [When we were out] he started … saying 'I can see the way he's looking at you, blah, blah' 'Oh, you're giving him a hug'. But I said, yeah he's my friend, you were with me, I'm introducing you … we went to the one pub, he seen one of my ex-boyfriends, knowing I was with him

just before I got with him. He's like, 'oh [your ex-boyfriend's] over there mmm', I was like, 'yeah and?' 'Well I've seen you say hi to him', 'well I'm not going to ignore him, he's never done nothing wrong to me'... he just ... was niggling all night and I knew what was gonna happen when I got home or when we got out of the pub that he was gonna hit me anyway. So the police drove past and I jumped in the middle of the road to stop 'em. I said...he's kicking off...can you just give me a lift home? [The policeman] said we ain't no taxi service, and...[was] basically gonna drive off and I just sat in the car and I refused to get out. And they said, no, no, no, dragged me out see, like in other words, we don't deal with domestics, they were saying. So, I did, I hit the copper because at the end of the day I knew if I went home it was gonna be worse .... So I got arrested for assault on a police officer, but I knew I was safer there than going home.

Donna's actions in these circumstances demonstrate how victims' nuanced knowledge of their abusers, and the actions they would take to inflict abuse, can inform and influence their coping strategies, and the subsequent actions they could or would take to avoid harm (see also Ferraro, 2006). Such actions can also reflect the limited options available for victims to escape or avoid abuse (in particular severe physical attacks). Donna's behaviour in this situation is contextualised by her statement: 'I knew what was gonna happen when I got home ... he'd pull my hair, drag me and stamp on me' which demonstrates her knowledge of her abuser's behaviours and the violence she knew would follow his actions when they were out. Donna's actions, in terms of her attempt to avoid/protect herself from a physical assault, corroborate Kelly's (1988) assertions regarding how women can respond to threats of violence. For example, Kelly (1988, p. 161) notes that

the threat of violence often results in anticipatory coping behavior through which women avoid ... violence. The effectiveness of chosen strategies may vary over the short and long term and coping may involve costs to the woman.

In Donna's case the cost of the strategy she adopted to avoid a physical assault was a criminal conviction but she stated

with the offences, like I said, I hit the police officer because that's my escape out .... I was doing it because, to protect myself basically. I'd rather be in a police station than go home to [my abusive partner].

Findings from another study also help contextualise Donna's actions. Ferraro's (2006) research identified how abuse victims' actions and means of coping with their abuse are informed by their expert and nuanced knowledge of their abuser which help them establish ways to avoid or prevent harm to themselves or others. As the United Nations (2013, p. 6) further corroborates:

> Threats of violence [or abuse] are sometimes explicit but may also be implied, for example manifesting in comments or actions that might seem insignificant to an outside observer but that may signal an imminent attack for a victim.

In Donna's situation her actions were motivated by her fear of her abuser and it could therefore be argued these fears exceeded her fear of the CJS (or more relevantly, the sanctions of the CJS). Her fears were evoked by her abuser's previous threats (such as his threats to kill her) and previous physical assaults and consequently influenced the actions she took to remain safe from harm. A woman's fear of her abuser exceeding her fears of the sanctions of the CJS is something that was also identified by Ferraro (2006, p. 203) who describes the all-consuming control a perpetrator of abuse can have over their victim:

> the coercion that occurs within intimate relationships ... involves every aspect of a woman's life. She is not only concerned about immediate consequences for failure to obey, but about the longer-term effects on her children, extended family, and her abusive partner. The tentacles of authority within abusive relationships have a much greater and more tangled reach than those of authorities who have no ties to their subject.

This perspective was further evidenced during interviews with multiple Probation staff members, who recognised that for victims of domestic abuse the punitive actions of the state, or criminal justice agencies, may not even be considered when responding to their victimisation, as the woman's sole objective is to simply stay alive:

> I think the law side of it probably doesn't even come into much of her thinking process ... the fear of him, or her (the [abusive] partner) probably far outweighs whatever else could be going on for them. (Probation staff member 13)

> When people are in a situation where their home life is so chaotic, dangerous ... the sanctions of the criminal justice system, in comparison with what they're actually dealing with are minor, so they're not worried about whether they're going to prison or whether they've got to go on an order or not, they're worried about whether they're gonna get killed. (Probation staff member 15)

The second Probation staff member elaborated on the need for the CJS to recognise such circumstances and suggested that understanding how domestic abuse can impact upon a woman should also have implications for how she is supervised:

> that is, you know, an extreme example [referring to the quotation above] but actually it's more common than we think, so, therefore what you're doing to try and address the offending, if that's [domestic abuse is] the real reason for the offending, is never gonna have any impact because, you know, you're saying oh well you shouldn't be doing this and so this is gonna be the punishment in order to put you off doing that but actually if what they're suffering is so much more serious than that, that is like a drop in the ocean to them and what we actually need to be doing is addressing those underlying reasons and giving them some hope that they can come out of that lifestyle, if we're ever gonna have any impact on them. (Probation staff member 15)

As these Probation staff members suggest, for women experiencing domestic abuse their actions are often primarily motivated and contoured by their responses to the abuse they are being subjected to or their reactions to their abusers. The consequences these actions may have *outside* of the abusive relationship and the immediate instinct to stay alive, particularly for women on orders or on licence, do not necessarily impact upon their thought processes, given the risk to their lives. This perspective is corroborated by Richie (1996) who identified that women experiencing abuse would often placate or acquiesce to the demands of their abusers, whether these actions were legal or not, as the risk of not doing as was asked/demanded by the abuser was far greater, including being severely physically assaulted or threatened with death (referring to either the woman's own murder or the murder of her children).

During the interviews, a further two women spoke about using prison as a route to escape domestic abuse, but in one of these cases this was just something that had been considered but had not yet been acted upon. Ellie, aged 21, revealed that she had experienced domestic abuse in a relationship with a boyfriend for a period of nearly 5 years and after this she had experienced domestic abuse perpetrated by her sister. She spoke about how she had considered prison as a means of escaping abuse

> If I reoffended myself then I would make sure I would go to prison to get away from that person [abuse perpetrator] and I would literally do anything to get myself locked up, so then I feel safe and obviously prison ain't the answer but ....

Skye, aged 23, was serving a sentence for aggravated burglary and had been in one abusive relationship which had lasted over a year. She spoke about how her time in prison had provided a physical separation from her abuser and enabled her to leave the relationship. Prior to her time in prison she had felt there was no other opportunity for escape:

[the abuse] kept on and on and on for a year and I thought, soon as I went to prison, I couldn't wait to go to prison, that's how bad it was, honest to God …. I thought there was no escape there, what-soever, not once, no escape, to get out of there [the abusive rela-tionship], the only escape I had to do was when I went to prison, that's the only escape.

Drawing upon their wealth of experience of supervising women, a number of the Probation staff members provided further anecdotal evidence of women utilising the CJS as a means of escaping experience of abusive relationships:

there [are] people who want to go to prison to remove themselves from the situation as well…they [commit] an offence … serious enough or persistent enough 'cause they know that when they go to prison it's their only place of safety and sanctuary and that they need some time out and even if they're going to return to the abuser they still needed that. (Probation staff member 6)

Women committing particular types of offences, or more serious offences, in order to be sentenced to custody as a means of accessing what they perceive to be safe and secure accommodation was also a tactic identified by probation staff member number 6:

I've also had [women] … that they said they knew they took an item off a person and it's a robbery offence they knew that would then shift them up in terms of, that it would be crown court and it would be more likely to get a custodial sentence because they were desperate to go back to custody 'cause that's the only place that they felt safe and secure, was in custody. (Probation staff member 6)

The tactic of intentionally committing crime to initiate being imprisoned was also recognised by Richie (1996) in her study of African American women who had experienced domestic abuse. Richie's research revealed cases where imprison-ment was viewed by some incarcerated women as one of the very limited routes to safety from abuse. Using jail as a safe option for accommodation to meet basic survival needs was a troubling trend described by the women she interviewed. Similarly to Charlie's statement that it was only when she was behind the steel prison door that she could '*finally breathe*', a number of participants in Richie's study also articulated their relief at being incarcerated as it was only at this point they found safety from years of being subjected to violence and abuse.

In addition to utilising imprisonment as a means of exiting an abusive rela-tionship, one probation staff member, drawing upon their experience of supervis-ing many female offenders, suggested that the consequences of leaving an abusive relationship may also contribute to a woman's desire to go to prison:

[the victim has] tried to leave the relationship ... or they've tried to move on and they've either been pulled back by the partner, or whatever the alternative is, is so bleak that they don't want to be in either, they don't want to be in an abusive relationship but they don't want to be out there on their own, independent. They're not used to living on their own, they're not used to functioning independently and they're missing all that intimacy and attachment and they're also struggling to deal with all the general life things, the bills and life and all the other problems that they didn't have when they were in a relationship. So they can't cope with either worlds, so the only world they can see that they can cope in is the prison world where it's all done for them and they just have to wake up and live and breathe. (Probation staff member 6)

This interview extract suggests that the levels of control some women are subjected to by their abusers can also have significant consequences for their ability to function *outside* of that relationship, demonstrating the wide-reaching, and long-term, consequences of being subjected to domestic abuse. Stark (2007, p. 274) refers to the significant levels of control exerted by perpetrators as the 'micromanagement of everyday life' where the freedoms denied to victims of domestic abuse are the '... taken for granted fabric of everyday affairs ...'. He also states that such high levels of control deprive women of any significant autonomy or freedom and, as a consequence, this results in women becoming unable to exert any form of 'choice'. Therefore, due to the depth and breadth of control that some women are subjected to within their abusive relationships, for some women who have experienced domestic abuse, it can be extremely daunting to live independently.

Elaborating upon the problematic consequences leaving abusive relationships can have for women, other academics have identified that women may also be concerned about the practicalities of leaving (Kirkwood, 1993) including having access to money and housing as well as the implications of living independently (see Abrahams, 2007). This is a result of the many aspects of normal social functioning, such as managing money and household bills, personal freedom (including gaining and/or maintaining employment) and self-dependency, which may have always been controlled or restricted by women's abusers. The actions of domestic abuse perpetrators in attempting to maintain control over all aspects of their victims' lives further limit and restrict their victims' options for survival outside of the abusive relationship. Therefore, for some women prison could be seen to provide an environment where the responsibilities of the outside world, such as finances and accommodation, continue to be subject to someone else's control. This perception can be easily understood when contextualised by the woman's experience of domestic abuse. As a result of the control enforced and the trauma experienced during their abuse consequently women may experience long-term psychological consequences affecting their ability to perform routine tasks meaning they may also lack the skills or ability to live independently (Gorde et al., 2004). Subsequently, after an abusive relationship has ceased survivors may experience difficulties in organising their own lives and making decisions for themselves and their families (Abrahams, 2010). As Abrahams (2010) identified, domestic abuse can often destroy all sense of self-worth in survivors and can diminish their self-belief and confidence. As a result, many of the women's worries, after having left their abuser, refer directly to how to function outside of this relationship including managing alone, living independently, and being able to make decisions both for themselves and their children. Consequently, the long-term impact upon women's self-esteem could subsequently manifest in a:

> [...] lack of confidence in themselves and their abilities ... [resultant] from the abuse ... [which after exiting the abusive relationship] meant a lot of anxious internal debate on what they should be doing and what were the best options. (Abrahams, 2010, p. 87)

As has been established within this chapter, for some women in abusive relationships, imprisonment or the process of being detained by police overnight, can facilitate a forced and complete separation from an abuse perpetrator, either temporarily or more permanently. Importantly, it could be argued that such actions provide a form of social commentary where the women's actions reflect upon the inadequacies of both criminal justice and community-based responses to domestic abuse which, in some cases, could be perceived as unable to provide women with the protection, safety, or support they need. This is a perspective shared by Kraft-Stolar, Brundige, Kalantry, Kestenbaum and Avon Global Centre for Women and Justice at Cornell Law School and Women in Prison Project (2011) who suggest that the failure to protect victims of domestic abuse places them in a position where they then must take action to manage/survive the abuse they are experiencing, actions which can subsequently result in their criminalisation. This theory is corroborated by Charlie's situation as she had accessed a range of services in the community, including refuge, but still feared severe physical assault or being murdered by her partner. Consequently, as Segrave and Carlton (2010, p. 295) state, such circumstances '...render imprisonment the only "alternative" option – the only way to interrupt cycles of abuse, addiction and/or financial pressure that leads to lifestyles focussed on survival'. One of the probation staff members interviewed for the study also elaborated upon the all-consuming nature of domestic abuse and why some women may use prison as an escape from this. She highlighted the perseverance of abuse perpetrators in maintaining contact with/control over their victim, explaining that compared to community-based support prison is one place where abusers simply cannot physically gain access to their victim:

> [...]even though there [are] support agencies out there to do it all, they [victims of domestic abuse] may have tried that and failed that because the abuser's always found them, or re-hooked them back in emotionally, but when you're in prison obviously the abuser can't ... they can still get to you via letters and contact, but they're physically removed from you in prison, it's the only one

place an abuser can't turn up and gain access in the middle of the night to somebody … even if they were moved into a refuge they can still get there and a lot of females use prison as an excuse and say well I can't make calls 'cause I've got no credit or you're not allowed a visit, when they really are allowed a visit you know, but they can't get away with that if they're in the community. (Probation staff member 6)

As this quotation demonstrates unlike the services that are available in the community where abuse perpetrators may still be able to gain access to their victims, (e.g., outreach services where the victim remains in her home, or refuge where women can in some cases be located by their abuser), imprisonment facilitates a secure physical separation. This forced and physical separation not only provides safety for women but, in some cases, the support provided to the woman or the distance from the perpetrator may contribute to the woman's decision to leave the relationship permanently.

At this point, it must be heavily emphasised that utilising imprisonment as a route of escape from an abuse perpetrator, or as a form of reprieve from an abusive relationship, does not reflect upon the distinctly negative impact that incarceration can have on women. When this route is taken by women who have been subjected to domestic abuse it does not suggest that prison has any positive or rehabilitative qualities, instead, as Segrave and Carlton (2010, p. 295) suggest 'prison is the only option rather than the desired option'. In these circumstances the women's actions may infer that the protection or support afforded to victims of domestic abuse within the community may not be sufficient enough to ensure their safety or survival. Importantly, any positive effects of taking this route must be tempered by acknowledgement of the numerous negative and harmful effects the process of imprisonment can have on women, including causing them further trauma. The negative impact of imprisonment on women has been widely discussed within existing literature (see Corston, 2007; HMIP, 2006; Carlen and Worrall, 2004; McIvor, 2004 and Carlen, 2002, 1998, 1983 to provide just some examples) including Segrave and Carlton's (2010) suggestion that prisons can dehumanise and infantalise women, causing significant harm. Segrave and Carlton (2010) also state that when women use imprisonment as a route out of domestic abuse at best this serves only as a 'stop gap' in the women's lives. Critically, what the women's actions do indicate, however, is the dangerous situations and circumstances that victims of domestic abuse are placed in by their abusers and the desperate actions the women feel they need to take to escape such abuse.

Chapter 7

Grace, Linda and Shayan: The Long-term Impact of Surviving Domestic Abuse on Women's Pathways into Offending

Grace was 49 years old when she was convicted of benefit fraud and she received a 24-month suspended sentence from the courts. This was her first offence and she had no prior involvement with the CJS. At the time of her interview Grace was in a new relationship, which she said was not abusive, but she had previously been married and had been subjected to domestic abuse by her ex-husband for 25 years. She had four children and her relationship with the three children she had with her ex-husband was extremely fractured as a result of his abusive behaviour and his desire to alienate Grace from them.

Like many women who have experienced domestic abuse, Grace described how the beginning of the relationship with her ex-husband had been good, but the abuse had begun when she had her first child:

> [The relationship] was fine, it was brilliant actually, until we had my daughter and then that's when it all went downhill … he didn't like her being first and then as she got older then he started using his fists a bit more. That I could cope with, it's the mind games I hated the most! Like I was ugly, fat, thick, stupid … that's how it got bad and then when I had my two sons it just [became] ridiculous then, especially with [son] being ill, because he had a bad heart and kidneys, so he was in and out of hospital. [Second son] had Von Willebrand's which is a bleeding disorder, again, in and out of hospitals …. So it just got worse and worse, I used excuses like the cat punched me, black eyes from a cat! I'm clumsy I fall over, a lot of stupid excuses!

Not only was Grace's husband physically and verbally abusive, he was also extremely controlling, as Grace elaborates:

Gendered Justice? How Women's Attempts to Cope With, Survive,
or Escape Domestic Abuse Can Drive Them into Crime, 51–64
Copyright © 2022 by Jo Roberts
Published under exclusive licence by Emerald Publishing Limited
doi:10.1108/978-1-80262-069-620221008

I weren't allowed friends, weren't allowed out, couldn't go shopping on my own. I could walk to the school and back and that's about it. Never, never went out. I joined a gym, big mistake, once, because I screwed everybody there apparently! Didn't matter if they were male or female and then when I worked at the school, I started getting work, and I worked with his sister in law, so I was having an affair with his brother, his sister-in-law, everybody! [He said I was] stupid and he said how can you work in the school you're too thick? So I used to try and point out that I actually had more exams than he did and higher! 'Cause you can't take that away, I did 'em, they were mine! ... he would use things like that, if I spoke to anybody, oh don't want you speaking to her, she's a slut, or you can't talk to her, she's too fat or you can't go with her, I know what she's like when she's out.

In Grace's case her involvement in crime appeared to be contextualised by her experiences of domestic abuse, although for Grace her involvement in crime occurred *after* she had left her abusive husband. Unlike many of the other women's accounts in the book (such as May's and Charlie's for example) Grace's actions were not an immediate response to a current abusive relationship. Instead, Grace's behaviour, which led to her benefit fraud conviction, could be described as a long-term consequence of the abuse she had previously been subjected to. Grace describes the circumstances related to her offence:

Well what happened is, I'm signing on [claiming benefits], and when I had [youngest daughter] [my new partner] used to come round, was meant to come round just two days a week to see her, well he could see her five days a week as long as he didn't stop over, but when I was ill, he'd stop over a couple of nights to have baby and then when she was coming up two [years old], he said well, we might as well just move in together but I didn't sign off straight away because it was like a safety net, I could chuck him out [gets emotional] I know it sounds awful, but I could chuck him out and I'd still be safe. Oh I'm horrible in' I? .... And that's where I went wrong, because I wanted to feel safe [crying].

As Grace explains the circumstances which led to her offence; she continued to claim benefits when her new partner moved into her accommodation as she wanted to retain some financial resources which would function as a 'safety-net' should she later need to escape him if he became abusive. Grace's actions, in this context, demonstrate that women's responses to experiencing abuse may continue far beyond the relationship with their abuser. Instead, women's responses to their victimisation can extend far further than their immediate responses to surviving domestic abuse, leading to more longitudinal survival techniques. This theory is supported by Kelly's (1988) work examining coping mechanisms employed by survivors of sexual abuse and other forms of violence against women which established that women utilise coping strategies at multiple different points which include during an assault/at the time of the abuse but also after the events have taken place (and this can include in the immediate aftermath but also over longer periods of time). As Kelly (1988) also identified sometimes only the threat or possibility of violence/abuse may trigger a woman's coping behaviour which they employ in an anticipatory context in order to protect themselves, which is arguably why Grace took the actions she did.

To further contextualise Grace's actions, she explained that during her previous relationship with her ex-husband she had been subjected to financial abuse and as a result she had no financial resources. When Grace did eventually leave she didn't have any money, possessions, or resources:

> I never had any money, [ex-husband] never gave me a penny, I left with nothing. When I left him, I had my clothes on, that was it. He'd ripped my jewellery off, out my ears, everything. I left with absolutely nothing and to this day he's never given me nothing of mine back. None of my Dad's possessions, when he died, that he'd left me. [My ex-husband] kept everything, baby photos, that's the hurtful thing, out of everything, he could keep, but I wanted some baby photos of my kids, because I loved them, I would die for 'em!

Therefore, in complete contrast to the circumstances Grace was in when she fled her abusive ex-husband, when she commenced a new relationship and her partner moved in with her, she acted to ensure she would have access to financial resources so that she could, if necessary, retain the opportunity to be independent. Although Grace stated that her new relationship was not abusive, it was clearly evident that her previous experiences had conditioned her responses to her new relationship, which could be described as a means of survival. Again, drawing upon Kelly's (1988) work, she contended that women who have been subjected to domestic abuse will maintain a distrust of men, feelings which function as a self-protective response to the trauma experienced in order to prevent further abuse. Grace's behaviours embody such theories demonstrating the longitudinal impact that a woman's experience of domestic abuse can have on her behaviour and actions including when in relationships which are not abusive. When Grace was asked what motivated her to continue claiming benefits when her new partner moved in with her, she said:

> [The benefits were a] safety net, just because I didn't know if he [current partner] was gonna [pause] a month he moved in and I was like everyday wondering ... I just thought I've just had a baby, is he gonna think oh she gets more attention. Is he gonna start on her? 'Cause he [ex-partner] did start on the little ones but I protected them soooo much, I was worn out protecting them. 5 minutes late home from school – where are they? Even when I knew where they were, it was like, no, it's OK, I told them they could go ... excuses, excuses. [Long pause] I used to say to the kids Dad's in a bad mood, go to your bedroom, go to bed, just be out of the way 'cause that way they don't get it, you get it [crying].

As Grace's recollection of events demonstrate it was the long-term consequences of her previous abusive relationship, resulting in a continuous struggle
for survival, that provide a clear context to the actions she took in her subsequent
relationship. In this interview extract Grace articulates her fears about her new
partner becoming abusive, concerns reflecting the reality of her last (and very
long-term) relationship which subsequently extended to her next relationship.
The timing of Grace's new partner moving in was also significant as Grace had
described how her abusive ex-husband's violence had started when Grace's first
child was a similar age to the child she had with her new partner, therefore, compounding Grace's worries about what might occur within her new relationship.
Drawing upon Susan Schechter's theories, referenced by Kelly (1988), Schechter
conceptualises that for women who have experienced domestic abuse the impact
for them manifests in a wide range of losses, two of which include loss of control
and loss of trust. How, and to what extent, such loses affect women's lives and
choices, Schechter argues, will vary and ultimately arise out of the complex interaction between the abuse experienced, the women's responses to the abuse and the
coping responses available to them (referenced in Kelly, 1988).[1] Applying Schechter's ideas to Grace's case, it could be argued that Grace's actions of continuing
to claim benefits were in response to both her loss of trust (in men due to her
relationship with her ex-husband) and control (over her financial resources when
in her abusive relationship). Therefore, Grace's actions could be seen to have been
taken to maintain control over her new circumstances (both psychologically and
financially) behaviours which were clearly affected by her previous experience of
abuse. As Kirkwood (1993) also notes, when involved in an abusive relationship
women's control over both their material and personal resources can often be
removed by the perpetrator of the abuse and can result in a loss of identity and
power for the women. It is therefore unsurprising that a consequence of such
abusive relationships can be women wishing to re-establish control in their lives,
one manifestation of this can include financial security. As Kelly et al. (2014)
suggest, one of the most significant concerns for women when attempting to re-
establish their lives after leaving an abusive relationship is financial security, most
specifically in regard to how economic resources influence survivors' 'space for
action' and the choices they are able to make in relation to their lives and their
subsequent relationships.

Grace's pathway into crime was heavily influenced by her desire to secure her
own financial security and to equip herself with economic resources (the benefits
she was claiming) to provide her with a much-needed safety-net should she wish
to exit her new relationship if her partner became abusive. When attempting to
understand Grace's motivations for the actions she took the already existing literature and theory outlined above reinforce the suggestion that Grace's pathway

---

[1]There is no date included in Kelly's reference to Schechter and this refers to personal
communication between. The conceptualisation referenced here, however, is later ech-
oed in Schechter's (1982) *Women and Male Violence: The Visions and Struggles of the
Battered Women's Movement.*

into crime both reflects and responds to her previous experiences of abuse which contoured and influenced the coping mechanisms she had subsequently developed to protect herself from future harm. This perspective is further corroborated by Root (1992) who identified that the realities women construct after an experience of trauma can feel far less safe or secure and as a consequence women become more aware of, or heightened to, possible threats to their safety. If employing Root's theory to Grace's situation it could be claimed that specific survival behaviours were activated by the situation Grace found herself in as a consequence of the abuse and trauma she had been subjected to by her ex-husband, resulting in a long-term impact on Grace's behaviour.

These ideas, suggesting that a woman's coping behaviours can be affected in a long-term context as a result of experience of abuse, are also similar to those of Comack (2000) who studied female prisoners and their pathways into crime. In her research Comack (2000, p. 94) identified that, for two of the women she spoke with, being subjected to domestic abuse had 'initiated a lengthy process of coping and adapting' which they employed both inside and outside of their abusive relationships. Furthermore, at the end of her study Comack (2000, p. 149) concluded that: 'For some women ... [their] law violation[s] were part and parcel of their ongoing struggle to survive the conditions of their endangerment'.

Further examples of the long-term impact of domestic abuse upon women's coping strategies and behaviours and how they can contribute to women's involvement in crime arose from the interviews with the women. Linda spoke about how her long-term coping mechanisms had led to her involvement in the CJS. At the time of her interview Linda was 54 years old, she had two grown up children and had been in two relationships. She had been in a relationship with her husband for 33 years but had separated from him when their children had become adults. After her relationship with her husband ended Linda became involved with another man and was with him for 6 years and it was this second relationship that she described as abusive. Linda spoke about how the relationship had started off well but quickly became characterised by her partner's abusive and controlling behaviour:

> The first year I was with him I thought all my Christmases and birthdays had come at one, he was a right charmer, looked after me, and then a friend of his owns a club and I was asked basically to run the club, because he had previous, he'd been to prison things like that, he couldn't have got a personal licence to run the club. So I'd never been in trouble, I went and I done the course and I got the personal licence I needed to run it and it was fine when we first started but then he started getting, he was really jealous. [His] jealousy was terrible! Nobody could even look at me and he was constantly watching everything I did, if I'd go shopping and then he'd say well how long you going to be? I'd say, oh, half hour, if I was 40 minutes he'd be pacing back and fore waiting for me and that's how it started. And then there was a row this one day that he's had with somebody in the, the club and he basically took it out on me.

> Erm, that was the first time that he ever hit me, which should have
> been the last really but I went back and kept going back and back
> again, erm, until in the end I just thought well this is the life that
> I'm going to have 'cause originally I honestly thought that I could
> be the one to change him 'cause when I first, I've known this man
> for 30 odd years, erm, and as I said he come across always a lovely
> fella, a right charmer, knew all my family, he used to work for my
> brother, when my brother was running [pub in town], he used to
> work on the door, for the big games and that, so very nice man.

Linda provided more detail about the abuse she had been subjected to by her
ex-partner which not only included physical abuse but controlling behaviours as
well:

> Well I couldn't go anywhere, I weren't allowed to go anywhere.
> As long as I was with him and he could watch every move and
> it just got that I … couldn't go anywhere on my own, we went to
> New York one Christmas and we ended up having a big row there
> because he slapped me round there because he said there was a
> fella looking at me when we was sat in the pub, he just spoiled eve-
> rything and after the first year he was so lovely and I knew what he
> could be like I honestly thought that I could get him to go back to
> it but it never worked. I still got feelings for him now.

When she took part in the study Linda had been convicted of drink-driving and had been sentenced to a 12-month suspended sentence order, she had
received a 48-month driving ban, had to complete a 12-month community order
being supervised by Probation and had to undertake some rehabilitation activity
requirements (RARs). Linda's offence took place a number of years after she had
left her abusive relationship, but her account suggested that the foundations of
her involvement in crime had been established by the abusive relationship she had
been in and the coping mechanisms she used to manage her experiences. Linda's
ex-partner, seemingly as a means of exerting control over her, had encouraged her
alcohol dependence, as she describes:

> Whereas I wasn't a drinker before I met him, you know, I never
> went out. I used to go to [seaside town] with the girls once a year
> and I'd have a boozy weekend and it'd take me a fortnight to get
> over it but … we were out every night and drinking every night
> and that's how basically the relationship went, it all revolved
> around drink and for, for 2 and half/ 3 years that's a lot of drink
> to build up in your system and then of course with the abuse and
> everything it just gets worse. Yeah, so everything revolved around
> drink in that relationship right up to my offence.

As Linda's account illustrates not only did her abusive partner actively encourage her alcohol consumption, when the abuse escalated and after Linda left the

relationship she began employing alcohol as a means of coping with what she had been through. When asked if she felt that the domestic abuse she was subjected to had contributed to her pathway into crime she responded:

> Oh definitely. Because of the drinking, because I never drunk before, very little and then it got when after the abuse, I felt that I didn't have anything else and it was my comfort story to myself basically, oh it's alright Linda, you can have a drink, have another one, have another one and that's how it got until in the end I just couldn't stop myself, I was drinking so much that I'd just pass out and I wouldn't remember. I'd get up the next morning, wouldn't remember what I'd done the night before.

Linda's means of managing the abuse she experienced culminated in her alcoholism which consequently led to her drink-driving offence. The foundations of her alcohol use were laid by her abuser who initially introduced and encouraged her excessive drinking, after which she then turned to alcohol to cope with the years of abuse she was subjected to and this coping mechanism continued after she had exited the relationship. The use of alcohol as a coping response employed by victims of domestic abuse was something identified by Downs and Miller (1994) in their longitudinal study which also found that alcohol use often increases when women are being subjected to domestic abuse. Alcohol or drug dependence employed as a coping mechanism for managing experiences of domestic abuse was also referenced by Women's Aid (2011). Like Linda, who described her use of alcohol as something which provided her with a sense of 'comfort', women's use of drugs or alcohol could be seen to be a way to escape their traumatic experiences. After the cessation of her abusive relationship Linda continued to use alcohol as a means of dealing with the relationship breakdown and her loneliness after her abuser had isolated her from her friends and family:

> I felt I didn't have anything else so I was drinking then more or less every night and then it got that I was drinking every night and I was taking it out on my family then because, because I was hurting I wanted everybody else to feel the pain that I was feeling and I was making them feel that pain by being vicious and horrible to 'em and then I'd cry my eyes out then because I was upsetting people and I'd be doing things that the next day I wouldn't even remember I'd done and it got that I, until after that drink drive, it got that I thought, oh that's, that was the kick that I needed to say you've gotta stop this.

Previous research such as Kaysen et al.'s (2007) has revealed an association between alcohol use and an individual's repeat exposure to incidents of interpersonal trauma, such as domestic abuse. They identified that using alcohol as a response to being subjected to different forms of trauma can be motivated by 'various coping-oriented reasons [such as] … to medicate sleep difficulties … to reduce negative effect … and psychological distress' (Kaysen et al., 2007, p. 1273). Linda's circumstances suggest that the long-term impact of the coping mechanism she employed for managing the abuse she was subjected to and the breakdown of her relationship contributed to her involvement in crime, therefore culminating in an indirect relationship between her experience of domestic abuse and her offending. Crucially, in addition to Linda's experience of domestic abuse shortly before her drink-driving conviction, she had also experienced other traumatic events; her brother had recently died, and her ex-husband began a relationship with another woman who was younger than their daughter. Therefore, in her case it appears that it was the cumulative effective of multiple psychologically distressing events which compounded her dependence upon alcohol, as she said '… all happened together and [I] just couldn't cope'.

Women involved with the CJS have often experienced multiple forms of trauma (Pemberton et al., 2019; Earle et al., 2014; Prison Reform Trust, 2014a; National Offender Management Service or NOMS, 2013; Women's Aid, 2011) and this was a phenomenon identified in DeHart's (2004) study of female offenders who had all experienced multiple traumas during their lives. DeHart highlighted how many women involved in the CJS have experienced different forms of victimisation such as childhood violence and domestic abuse, which are characterised by their repeat nature, leading her to label such experiences 'poly-victimisation'. DeHart (2004, p. vii) argued that these multiple experiences of trauma could have a distinct effect on women's lives:

> […] the varied impacts of poly-victimisation have potential to create ripple effects in multiple arenas in the women's lives, causing overall disruption and pushing women out of the mainstream. Often, the intersection of events and losses seemed to create uniquely difficult situations.

Therefore, using DeHart's theories and applying them to Linda, her pathway into crime could arguably be contextualised by her multiple experiences of trauma and loss which evoked her coping response, her use of alcohol, and subsequently contributed to her pathway into crime when she got behind the wheel of a car under the influence of alcohol. It was the long-term coping response that Linda had employed throughout her abusive relationship that spilled into her behaviour after she had left this relationship that led to her involvement in crime. Conclusively Linda's involvement in crime could be described as a by-product of the domestic abuse she was subjected to and the other traumas she had to cope with. To elaborate, her drink-driving offence did not result from a deliberate choice to break the law, instead her alcoholism manifested as a consequence of the domestic abuse she was subjected to and the mechanisms she needed to employ to survive the abuse. Women's Aid (2011) also point to the negative consequences that certain coping responses can have for women as they note that in the short term the use of substances may provide relief or comfort, however, in the longer term the impact of such coping mechanisms can be problematic.

This chapter will conclude with one further example of the long-term impact that the coping mechanisms women employ to manage the abuse they experience can have on their pathways into crime. In connection with Linda's case, Shayan's offence also occurred *after* she had exited an abusive relationship and was not the result of an immediate response to domestic abuse; instead her actions can be attributed to her *past* experiences of abuse.

When she was interviewed for the study Shayan was 38 years old and had three children. She had been convicted of assault occasioning Actual Bodily Harm (ABH) and had been sentenced to a 12-month community order. This was not her first offence and her OASys record noted that both relationship issues and issues of emotional well-being had been identified as contributing to her offending. Shayan described all of the relationships she had been in from a young age as abusive with the two most significant abusive relationships lasting 11 years and 5 years, respectively. Shayan, however, felt that the abusive relationship which lasted over a decade was the most relevant to explaining her pathway into crime. Shayan described the abuse she was subjected to during her relationship with her ex-husband:

> I was with him for 11 years and he subjected me to 11 years of domestic abuse .... It was mental abuse, sexual abuse, financial, I was financially controlled. There were injuries, my nose, he broke my nose many a time, so I had to have it re-set, bust my eardrum, cracked my hip, scolded me in hot water, in like a boiling bath, over the years it was really bad. But I always say it's the mental abuse that's the worst, he'd lock me out to sleep with the dog and do stuff like that. But one of the worst things was he wouldn't let me take the contraceptive pill, and 'cause when I'd been a child and I'd also grown up seeing violence, I didn't wanna put children through this anymore and at the age of 25 the only way I could stop having children, the only like contraception he would allow me was to be sterilised, which inevitably took my chance to have children away from me forever, so that's a bit sad like.

As Shayan's description of her relationship with her husband illustrates, she was subjected to a wide range of forms of abuse for over an 11-year period. Not only did Shayan's ex-husband physically and sexually abuse her, he also isolated her from her family and friends leaving her with no support network:

> I weren't allowed no friends ... the only friends I was allowed they were partners of his friends .... But yeah my family ... he fought with my mother and he fought with my brother and they were just trying to look out for me and come and get me away from him, when they'd be like that or, trying to say to me, look he's bad news, he would turn around you know in my head, and make out like, oh they don't like you 'cause of this and they don't like you because

of that and because you're so weak at the time, you just can't see what's happening, a little bit of you do believe it. Well I believed everything for the whole 11 years, it was only afterwards I was like, oh my God! I can't believe it!

Shayan eventually left her husband when he was sent to prison and she committed her offence a number of years later. She describes what took place:

[…] just instantly inside me I thought No! Hang on a minute, my children have seen this [domestic abuse], all these years and I feel, I felt, I've always felt guilty about that, but my children have seen this all these years and I'm not having another man subjecting them to that, again. So, like, automatically in my head it was there, I'm going to hit him, something, I'm gonna do something, I'm not going to let him get away with this.

Shayan committed a crime when she assaulted a man whom she knew to be violent and abusive. Within the study Shayan's crime was labelled as a form of 'subversion', in other words, her involvement in crime could be perceived to be an attempt to reject the imbalance of power she was subjected to within her abusive relationship, enacted as means of taking back a form of control. Shayan did not commit this act against her own abuser, as she may not have had the power to do so at that time. Instead years later, when confronted with another abusive man who was committing violence in front of her children, she took action. Shayan provides further context to her offence:

she's [sister in-law] like had men that have been horrible to her in her time and she's always tried to do the best for her children and I think, so little bit of her she reminds me of me, she's like a tough girl and she deserved a bit better and her children, I love her children to bits even now they still come down the house … they would come and tell me, oh he's doing this to my Mammy, he's doing that to my Mammy, and I was thinking to myself … I suppose it was just the fact that, the tipping point of it … [the abuse of my sister-in-law] happened in front of my daughter and I think it was because only once my daughter ever witnessed [domestic abuse] … with him [my ex-husband] … something's just gone ping in my head right, 'cause I'm thinking is it something to do with like women? … 'cause my daughter have seen it, even though my sons had seen it all that time, soon as, the moment my daughter had seen it I was like no, I'm not having my girl seeing it and then she's seen it in front of another bloke and that's tipped me over the edge. But I think perhaps I'm just protective over … the women … the female part of it and I'm thinking that a female isn't weaker than a man like and just trying to show that.

When contextualised by her experience of domestic abuse Shayan's actions can be interpreted as a delayed response to the abuse she herself had experienced which she enacted against someone symbolic of her abuser; another man whom she knew to be abusive. The actions that she took when she committed ABH could be viewed as a means of subverting her former status as a victim via taking back power from someone who perpetrates abuse and could also be seen to be a further response to her previous inability to take action within her former abusive relationship. The actions taken by Shayan which brought her into conflict with the law are highly symbolic and can be firmly traced back to her experiences of domestic abuse. They are symbolic in that her sister-in-law's situation mirrored Shayan's own previous situation as her sister-in-law was also a mother of three children and being subjected to domestic abuse and Shayan may have seen her own life reflected in her sister-in-law's. Even the weapon that Shayan used in the assault was symbolically significant; she used a saucepan to physically assault her sister-in-law's partner and for Shayan this was representative of the frequent times she had been attacked in the kitchen. She explained 'the worst part of the abuse was at home … little things like cooking … he'd come behind me and grab me by the hair'. Shayan elaborated upon why she chose this particular weapon:

> Little bit of me as well, which I never admitted because I think this is a bit pre-meditated, a little bit of me … I picked the saucepan up because I thought to myself ……and I've thought, you know like the cooking thing, I thought like while he was attacking me while I'd be cooking … is all I ever had to do … while I stood there cook-ing was pick a saucepan up and whack him on the head with it and then he would have stopped. Which, I know it's wrong, but just to protect myself from that and a little bit of me took that saucepan that day to try and show her [sister-in-law] look, when he's filling you in, in the house or something, just pick a saucepan up and hit him with it and that's it then, you're gone.

As Shayan's account demonstrates the situation in which she committed her crime triggered specifically traumatic memories for her which arguably initiated her coping responses. Importantly these coping responses were not enacted against her own abuser but were evoked when her daughter witnessed domestic abuse. The quotation above suggests that the crime Shayan committed was a symbolic enactment of actions she was unable to take within her 11-year abusive marriage. It could also be proposed that her actions were triggered in response to feelings of guilt and anger Shayan carried from her marriage regarding her children experi-encing domestic abuse where she was unable to remove them from that situation. This inability to escape or act out against her own abuser is therefore displaced and re-directed via attacking someone symbolic of her ex-husband. The catalyst to Shayan's actions could also be perceived to be abuse taking place in front of her daughter which also suggests that the situation triggered her protective instincts as she no longer wanted her children to experience abusive behaviours which are further reinforced by her statement:

> I think that because I know how much it, domestic abuse, affected
> me as a child, how much it's affected me as an adult, how much
> it's affected my children, from them witnessing it ... if I know that
> someone else is subjected, a woman or partner, to that and chil-
> dren it just like it makes me just want to stop it ... I see perpetra-
> tors of domestic violence – they['re] the weak ones, it's not the
> victim, they're the ones that are weak and I know by hitting them
> it's not the way to teach 'em, to me it's like, that's the way that they
> control everybody else, so I just think, right, hang on a minute,
> let's see how you likes it. 'Cause this is what you were doing to
> people and it's not just like, your hit is not just hurting that person
> ... it's also having a ripple effect throughout a lot of peoples' lives.
> So I just, that's how I feel but I just, react the wrong way I suppose.

Therefore, Shayan's actions could read as a rebellion not only against the abuse she was subjected to but also against the abuse of her children as well as women's collective experience of abuse. Interestingly, as this interview extract illustrates, Shayan's behaviour also reversed the role of victim and perpetrator, controlled and controller, as a consequence the actions she took both literally and symbolically subvert her role of victim/survivor by removing the abuser's ability to retain the power and control in that particular situation. Therefore although indirectly, and years after her own experiences of domestic abuse, it could be argued that the coping mechanisms that Shayan employed, that were triggered in response to the abuse of someone else, relate to her past experiences of violence and abuse. Shayan's situation therefore suggests that there is a longitudinal impact that a woman's experience of domestic abuse can have related to the 'psychological legacy of victimisation' (Rumgay, 2004, p. 4) which subsequently affected her pathway into crime.

In her study Richie (1996) also identified cases where victims/survivors of abuse retaliated against or attacked individuals symbolic of their own abusers and this brought them into contact with the CJS. In the pathways into crime that Richie established 'path two: projection and association' presented crimes women committed which were directed at 'men other than the batterer in a symbolic or projected retaliation for past abuse' (Richie, 1996, p. 110). Like Shayan's situation, all of the examples of path two that Richie included in her book also demonstrated the long-term consequences that a woman's experience of domestic abuse can have on women's pathways into crime. Richie's examples highlighted how, years after experiencing abuse, women's behaviours could be triggered in response to frustration, anger, and emotional damage which had been established via the abuse the women had been subjected to. In their work Street et al. (2005) also identified how a woman's long-term behaviours and how she responds to certain situations could be influenced and conditioned by her previous experiences of domestic abuse. They assert that '... traumatic sequelae are never "erased" and may re-emerge in the contexts similar to the original traumatic event' (Street et al., 2005, p. 246). Both Richie's (1996) and Street et al.'s (2005) findings therefore further validate the theory that Shayan's behaviour, when she committed the offence of ABH, can be attributed to her past experiences of domestic abuse and that her actions were affected by the long-term impact this abuse had upon her and her coping responses. The long-term impact of abuse or trauma on women's actions was also mentioned by this probation staff member who also references how coping behaviours can be triggered even after the trauma has ended:

> When someone experiences trauma [domestic abuse] then everyone responds to trauma in different ways depending on their own socialisation, their own personality, their own skills, their own resources available to them and some people kind of respond to trauma immediately and some people might not respond to it until years after the event, until something else maybe triggers it off, so I think the trauma's linked to the offending because it's usually a coping mechanism to deal with the trauma. (Probation staff member 6)

The probation staff member also further elaborated upon the long-term consequences of a woman's experience of domestic abuse, as she felt that even when the woman has exited that relationship her past experiences may also influence her involvement in crime:

> [...] if they are out of the relationship it doesn't necessarily mean that the actual relationship is causing it [the offending], it's the damage that the relationship's caused, so you could be in or out of the relationship, it's irrelevant sort of sometimes, usually it's probably more risk when you're out in terms of re-offending, than when you're in, 'cause when you're in, you're probably not re-offending as much, you're just living that trauma. (Probation staff member 6)

Finally, other studies have referenced the long-term impact that experiencing abuse can have on women's behaviours and actions which can manifest in situations long after the abuse has ceased. This research includes Root's (1992, p. 246) which states that:

> After a traumatic experience, one is more likely to be sensitive to threatening cues in the environment that are associated with the original trauma, or, through a process of higher-order conditioning, as associated indirectly.

Ferraro's (2006) work also refers to the impact of the perpetrator's 'gaze' on women's behaviour which references a victim's internalisation of their abuser's commands and control which is accompanied by the victim's policing of their own behaviour in order to always comply with the abuser's demands. Ferraro contends that this 'gaze' has a continuous and long-term impact upon women's behaviours which can be enacted when the abuse perpetrator is not present, when they are in prison and even after the abuser's death, as it is so indoctrinated into the victim's behaviours. The fear conditioning that victims have been subjected to therefore limits and shapes women's actions in a long-term context.

Conclusively therefore, when attempting to understand the ways in which a woman's experience of domestic abuse can influence a woman's involvement in crime it is important to explore the women's actions outside of their immediate responses to their victimisation and instead examine the longer-term impact that a woman's experience of domestic abuse can have on her behaviour. Importantly, the cases included in this chapter demonstrate that a woman's pathway into crime can be affected in a much broader context than is usually understood when examining the relationship between a woman's experience of domestic abuse and her involvement in crime. Rather than women simply offending with or against their abuser, or as a result of coercion enforced by them, instead women can commit crimes without the abuser being present, after exiting an abusive relationship or many years after the relationship and abuse has ended yet their behaviours and actions can still be attributed to their experience of domestic abuse.

Chapter 8

Sian, April and Mary: How Perpetrators of Domestic Abuse Employ the Criminal Justice System as a Weapon of Abuse

Sian was 31 at the time of her interview and she had been subjected to domestic abuse within three different relationships, this included when she was with her first boyfriend, her ex-husband, and during her relationship with her most recent partner whom she became involved with shortly after she had separated from her husband. She had four children and two were in her care at the time of the study. She had her first two children with her first partner and her second two children during her second relationship. Sian had left school early but had since completed an National Vocational Qualification (NVQ) in business.

Sian's abusive relationships had taken place over a period of 14 years, 8 of which she spent with her ex-husband. She described the level of control exerted within these relationships and the impact this had on her life:

> I've had 14 years of abusive relationships so I don't know who I am. I went from being a child and controlled by my parents and told what I could and couldn't do to 14 years of having a man telling me what I can and can't do.

The abuse Sian had been subjected to included physical, emotional, financial and sexual abuse, and was often accompanied by controlling behaviour.

At the time she was interviewed Sian had been convicted of benefit fraud (Social Security Offences) and this was her first and only offence. She had been sentenced to a 12-month community order accompanied by a curfew enforced from 6pm to 6am. The results of her OASys assessment recorded on her probation file confirmed that the Probation Officer allocated to supervise Sian had recognised that she was a survivor of domestic abuse. Her probation file also noted that Sian's victimisation had been identified as a contributory factor to

Gendered Justice? How Women's Attempts to Cope With, Survive,
or Escape Domestic Abuse Can Drive Them into Crime, 65–73
Copyright © 2022 by Jo Roberts
Published under exclusive licence by Emerald Publishing Limited
doi:10.1108/978-1-80262-069-620221009

her offence. When asked, Sian felt that her experience of domestic abuse had impacted upon her pathway into crime, stating:

> I think to be honest there was only the fact that I was in a situation
> I felt I had no escape from that caused [the offence] to be commit-
> ted in the first place.

To expand upon Sian's case; Sian's abusive ex-husband had constructed a set of circumstances which culminated in a criminal conviction for her, all as a result of his deliberate and sustained abuse. Sian describes the actions that her ex-husband took which she perceived had led to her involvement in the CJS:

> I had a report that I'd been accused of benefit fraud and [my ex-hus-
> band] did admit…that it was him who had reported it … because
> he was seen continuously coming in and out of the property, with
> keys [that he had stolen], it looked like he was still living there.

Sian's offence took place after she had fled her abusive ex-husband and she was living alone with her children in a Housing Association property, claiming single parent benefits. Sian's description of the events that led to her conviction illustrates how after she had left her abusive relationship with her ex-husband he had employed the CJS as a further mechanism of abuse, cultivating a set of circumstances in which it appeared that Sian was guilty of benefit fraud. Sian elaborates on these circumstances:

> Initially I wasn't with my husband but he was continuously turn-
> ing up to my property, if I'd pick the kids up from school he'd push
> his way through the door as I got there, he wouldn't leave for days
> on end, he'd steal my house keys so that he could let himself in and
> out … he'd help me out with things … because his credit rating
> was okay and [he said] 'well take out a catalogue, do it in my name,
> as long as I can order bits here and there then that's fine' [and]
> because our bank account was joint, although his address was at
> his mum's mine was to the [Housing Association] house, [this] all
> linked in with the benefit fraud then because they were saying well
> no, he has got things registered to this address.

Not only did Sian's ex-husband contact the police to report the alleged ben-efit fraud, his abusive behaviours established a set of circumstances in which Sian appeared guilty of committing the crime. Sian outlined further ways her ex-husband created the circumstances which led to her conviction:

> he signed his car over to me … but he never gave me the log books
> or anything, I never signed for the car, see he kept saying to me,
> it's my car, I'm lending you my car, I'm being nice, I'm letting you
> have it so it was like well okay he's got the works van but he is

trying to help me out, so in my mind I'm thinking credit where credit's due but it was all just games to be honest. It actually surprised me how manipulative people can be.

Sian's account of what had taken place demonstrates how she had endeavoured to re-build her life, via living independently with her children, after separating from her husband. Sian's attempt to escape the relationship, however, was met with her ex-husband's retaliatory actions, arguably taken to reinstate his power and authority or indeed to try to re-establish the relationship. Therefore, Sian's attempt to subvert the imbalance of power that she had been subjected to was responded to with a stronger reprisal by her ex-husband who employed the CJS as a means of punishing her for trying to leave him. Sian's ex-husband's actions are similar to those identified by Wilcox (2006, p. 24) who noted that

> It [is] when women decided to seriously and overtly resist being controlled that the men [abuse perpetrators] increased their levels of abuse/violence in order to reinstate and maintain their notion of 'social order'.

Wilcox's theory of abuse perpetrators acting to maintain their version of social order is reflected in the actions of Sian's ex-husband as they can be interpreted as an attempt to force Sian back into the relationship, using the CJS as a mechanism to facilitate this. Sian corroborates this by describing why she thought her ex-husband took the actions he did:

> It wasn't so much as to hurt me, it was to try and keep me with him because he knew if I had no money then I would, in his opinion, I would be with him. He even tried using the kids with it as well because he'd tell me that if we couldn't be a normal family, he was gonna contact social services, he was going to get the kids removed from me, they'd live with him instead, so it was anything and everything. He wasn't interested in the kids...he wanted me and that what's all of it has been about, having that control over me and stopping me escaping from him and he used everything in his power to do it and that was, the benefit fraud was one of the big things he used.

Sian elaborated upon her ex-husband's actions which she perceived were motivated by his desire to force her back into the relationship by interfering with her financial independence:

> [...][his actions were] just to try and make me financially dependent on him because if they stop my money, then I would have to go back to him and it was just more like harassment; it was just non-stop with him. Literally physically and emotionally draining ... in the middle I got a life-time restraining order against him ...

he doesn't know where I am, so, I'm a little bit more protected now but it is literally the extent I had to go to, to get away from him was beyond a joke.

The actions taken by Sian's ex-husband clearly demonstrate how perpetrators of domestic abuse can utilise the CJS as a weapon of abuse. As Sian illustrated, via the employment of physical, emotional and financial abuse, her ex-husband actively created a set of circumstances in which it looked as if Sian had been unlawfully claiming benefits. Sian's case also depicts the all-consuming nature of the domestic abuse she was subjected to highlighting the difficulties that survivors of abuse encounter when attempting to leave their relationships. Instead of Sian becoming involved in crime as a means of trying to escape abuse (like the cases discussed in Chapter 8) Sian's involvement in crime manifested as a result of her abuser employing the CJS as a mechanism to both punish her for leaving the relationship and a means of drawing her back into the relationship via removing her financial independence.

Unlike the previous chapters which have focussed upon actions taken by women who have been subjected to domestic abuse which have led to their involvement in crime, this chapter instead centres upon the actions of perpetrators of domestic abuse who employ the CJS itself as a weapon of abuse or a means of exerting power and control over their victims. April's case provides yet another example of how abusers can use the CJS as a mechanism of domestic abuse. At the time of her interview April was 44 years old and had been divorced for a number of years. During the interview she described how she had been in an abusive relationship with her ex-husband for 15 years. They had started a relationship when she was around 15 years old and still in school and she described them as childhood sweethearts. They quickly got married and had a daughter together. At the time of her interview April was in a new relationship and was recounting her experiences of domestic abuse retrospectively.

April's husband had been in the army for many years and after he left he started working as a policeman. April described how her husband had been incredibly controlling and emotionally abusive from very early in their relationship but that it had taken time for her to recognise his behaviour as abuse:

In the beginning, it was just, it was just telling me how to think and what to do but you don't see it. It's only when you look back you think, oh my god, didn't I have a mind of my own, how could everybody else see and I couldn't? But you just ploughed along then don't you for the kids and stuff, then you think that it's you.

April disclosed that her husband had become sexually abusive and had raped her whilst they were on holiday after which she became pregnant:

The last time [he was sexually abusive] was when we was [out of the UK], we went on holiday and he was ... I wasn't gonna go and it was like I've gotta go, my daughter was so excited, and we went away and things just got so out of hand and I come back and I was pregnant as a result of it, [very upset] but I couldn't go through with it, so I had a termination then ....

After the rape April left her ex-husband and it was at this point that he utilised his position of power, working within the CJS, as a way to locate her when she fled their home with their daughter to access refuge. April explains the circumstances when her ex-husband tried to locate her:

> [...] he tried to make out I kidnapped her [my daughter], now how can you kidnap your own child? You know, it was all done [me leaving] through the domestic violence unit, they were the ones who said, look it's unsafe for you to stay here .... But they just said it wasn't safe for me and she [police woman] got me out of there, soon as she could and then of course because I'd actually stood up for myself then, I wasn't letting him tell me that you're not going anywhere, you've gotta stay here, that he just tried to have me for kidnap and it was just all nonsense.

April's situation highlights how her ex-husband employed his position as a policeman to exploit the CJS as a weapon of abuse primarily to stop her from exiting the abusive relationship. His position of authority, as a criminal justice practitioner, and his access to the tools of the CJS, allowed him to utilise the system as a means of trying to continue to control her or perhaps punish her for leaving him. As April's case clearly demonstrates attempting to flee an abuser who is part of law enforcement can be exceptionally difficult given their 'unique' access to information which can result in them being able to locate refuges or their victims (see Yamamoto and Wallace, 2007). April's disempowered position was also further exacerbated by her inability to report her ex-husband's long-term abuse to the police as her husband was part of that institution. As Yamamoto and Wallace (2007) therefore note victims of domestic abuse perpetrated by police occupy unique positions of 'powerlessness' where the abuser, within their role as law enforcement, are well-known and respected in the local community as well as by their police colleagues, all of which deters victims from reporting the abuse. Fortunately, despite her ex-husband's attempts to instigate April's criminalisation, no further actions were taken:

> No [I wasn't charged], I just got taken to the police station with ... the woman who was working in the refuge and she just ripped them apart basically, she just told them they was being stupid and all this was to try and find out where I lived because all they wanted, they wanted me to give an address of where I was staying and it was like, no!

Although this particular situation was only briefly mentioned by April it is important to include as both hers and Sian's situations demonstrate how the CJS can be employed by perpetrators of abuse as yet another mechanism of domestic abuse.

A final example of perpetrators employing the CJS as a weapon of abuse included perpetrators' use of the courts or the police service as a medium through which they would accuse their victims of actually perpetrating the abuse, which is what happened to Mary. Mary was also 44 at the time of her interview and she had two adult children. She had met her husband at school and had completed her education after she finished her O-Levels. Mary had been with her now ex-husband for over 20 years and had been subjected to domestic abuse throughout the relationship. Mary described the range of abuse (physical, emotional, and financial) which her ex-husband had subjected her to during the two decades of their marriage:

> he battered me every day of the week but then it got to the stage where I was walking on egg shells, as soon as I heard him pulling up it's be like have I done the washing properly, have I done this right, have I done that right ... I used to have a little job which I thoroughly enjoyed but then he'd pick me up from work to make sure I went straight home. If the girls [from work] were going out for an evening ... I'd have to phone up, make an excuse, I couldn't go and oh well the kids were ill or and in the end they stopped asking me to go out with them .... With [my] clothes, he picked my clothes, had to have my hair the way he wanted me to have my hair. Eat what he told me to eat, my friends walked in the room, he'd walk upstairs, which is very uncomfortable and in the end they all just stopped coming round and then he'd be saying that my friend was like trying to hit on him and, and they're not my friends really and so in the end it was like ... he dominated absolutely everything in the end, and I couldn't have a bank account.

As Mary's recollection of her experiences clearly demonstrate, her ex-husband controlled all aspects of her life and he also subjected her to regular physical abuse, as she describes:

> I think the worst one [incident] was when he put a pillow over my face and well my lips were blue and he just pulled the pillow off and started laughing 'cause it's just a big joke, I couldn't breathe, and that was very, very scary. Like the punches and the burns and things like that, it's done but when you really think you're gonna die, and he's just sat there laughing at you ... if I wanted to go to the doctors, I couldn't go and see a doctor on my own he had to be in the room so I couldn't tell a doctor what was going on. Couldn't go to a dentist 'cause if I went to the dentist that's having an affair because he's gotta put his hands in your mouth .... He had to be everywhere, every anti-natal appointment, didn't miss any of them. If I was just going for like an examination after the

baby was born he had to be there and, just in case I told somebody, he'd have to be everywhere with me.

Mary had been convicted of common assault, this was her first and only offence, and at the time we spoke she was serving a 12-month community order. Her pathway into the CJS resulted from her (then) husband's accusation that she had been abusive towards him. She explains the circumstances relating to her offence which took place after she had left him:

> Well we were having a drink in my house, like friends come over, and he just turned up at the house and started being abusive towards me and my friend was there and she said, you know, just leave her alone, and then I went to go up the stairs, I can't remember, because I will admit, I was a bit drunk, but I went to go up the stairs and she said he pulled me back from the stairs and started right in my face, and she said you just lost it and she said you hit him ... but then on his statement he told the police he wasn't in my house, he ripped all my jacket ... all my hair, where he'd pulled my hair, was pulled out of the bobble, and my friend had made a statement saying what he had done and he denied all that and then about half hour after that they came out and said we've got to arrest you for battery. I said, you serious? Yeah he's making a charge against you. I said he can't do, I said he shouldn't have been in my house ... but we've got to, he's made a complaint against you, so had to spend the night in the police cell, was out the next day, and then had to go to court, obviously I went in refuge but then had to travel from here ... I pleaded guilty anyway, because I did it, I'm not gonna lie, and the solicitor said, well you're honest, I said well I did do it, you know ... I had to attend a 10-week course here, which I've completed and I got probation for 12 months and then £145 costs I had to pay.

When asked about her thoughts on what happened Mary concluded:

> I took it [domestic abuse] for nearly 20 years and only lashed out once, I mean there's women that take a lot more than what I've taken ... but they could end up stabbing somebody and they're the ones sent to prison...I blew once and then I got into trouble for it, but even the police were saying because he'd made [an accusation] ... which is fair enough, they've got to [investigate] ... you know, if I'd made a complaint against somebody and they said we'll just leave it then, I'd be annoyed as well, if they're just doing their job, but he done it to punish me ... 'cause I hit him back he's thinking, oh hang on a minute she's got the last, she's not having the last say now and that's why he went all the way to the courts.

Situations such as Mary's, where the abuse perpetrator accuses the victim of perpetrating the abuse, was recognised by one of the probation staff members as a way some women become involved in the CJS:

> We have a small number of people that, and I think it's a small number but actually I think it may be more common than maybe we realise, where actually women end up before the courts for violence towards male partners who are actually more violent towards them. So [victims] actually sometimes end up being before the court because that's another aspect of control that the man may have over them whereas they [the victims] would ordinarily, would never be brave enough to take that action against the man. In a way that's sort of the height of being a victim, of victimisation then isn't it, because we're actually dealing with people for being perpetrators of a crime that they're really the victim of. [It] flips the whole thing on to its head and it's really, really difficult to deal with. (Probation staff member 15)

As Mary's case, and the probation staff member's interview extract, demonstrate some perpetrators of abuse would accuse their victims of violence, assaults or abuse and use the CJS as a further weapon of their own abuse, which is what the probation staff member describes as 'the height of being a victim'. In cases such as this the CJS can actually further victimise survivors of abuse by punishing them for a crime which they have actually been the victims of. This type of victimisation is compounded by the woman's inability to have been able to report the crimes that she had been subjected to, often over a long time period (as in Mary's case).

Abuse perpetrators threatening to report their victims to statutory bodies is something that has been acknowledged within previous research. There is a wealth of literature which has highlighted domestic abuse perpetrators' use of reporting their victims to children's/social services or the department of work and pensions (DWP) as a means of controlling or punishing them (see Domestic Abuse Intervention Programs, 2011; Hester et al., 2007; Craven, 2005; Humphreys and Thiara, 2002; Richie, 1996). The Duluth Power and Control Wheel (Domestic Abuse Intervention Programs, 2011), a resource which outlines a range of tactics employed by abusers, includes 'threatening to report her [the victim of domestic abuse] to welfare' as an example of coercive and controlling behaviour exhibited by perpetrators of abuse.

The threat of being reported to children's services with the possible consequence of having children removed from the mother's care is a well-acknowledged form of controlling behaviour utilised by perpetrators of domestic abuse and was an area identified in my previous research (see Roberts, 2006). One of the women interviewed for this earlier study talked about how she had been accused of child neglect as a result of indirect threats made by her partner, as she explains:

> [...] my children got injured by the heater and got burnt and I got scared 'cause I was going to take them to hospital, to seek medical assistance, but he [my abusive partner] told me that if you take them to the hospital social services will come and take your child away, because from his previous marriage from his ex-wife and his other children, he had social services involved and had all these stories about what they [social services] did and what they're like so he really scared me, so I never actually took the kids to the hospital, just dealt with the injuries as best as I can. (Roberts, 2006, p. 83)

As this woman's situation demonstrates, an abuse perpetrator is able to control a victim's behaviour simply through an indirect threat, just mentioning the possibility of children being removed from their partner's care. In their research Humphreys and Thiara (2002) identified that tactics such as this could be deliberately employed by perpetrators of domestic abuse as a means of maintaining power and control over their victims. In direct comparison with perpetrators of domestic abuse employing the involvement of children's services as a mechanism of abuse, this study identified how abuse perpetrators would replicate this instead using the CJS. Therefore, actions such as threatening to report abuse victims to police, probation or escalate accusations to the courts were tactics clearly identified as further weapons of domestic abuse which could be used to manipulate, control, or punish victims.

Chapter 9

Summer and Skye: How a Woman's Experience of Domestic Abuse Can Affect Her Ability to Carry Out Her Sentence in the Community

> I had probation but I weren't attending because of my [abusive partner] 'cause I was too scared to go to town because, if I went to town I'd go back home and he'd hit me … and say … what was you in town for so long? I've been timing you. (Skye)

The narratives of the women involved in this study indicated that a woman's experience of domestic abuse can have much wider implications for her interaction with the CJS, outside of simply affecting her pathway into crime. Some of the women interviewed described how their experiences of domestic abuse could also impact upon their ability to carry out their sentences in the community. This finding is of particular importance for those working within the criminal justice sector given the implications for the management and support of women serving their sentences in the community.

It is important to note that although it was only a small number of the women who were interviewed that indicated their experience of domestic abuse had affected their ability to comply with their sentence, this likely reflects the smaller number of women that disclosed *current* experience of domestic abuse at the time of their interview. When the study took place most of the women who took part had already left their abusive relationships and were therefore recollecting their experiences retrospectively, hence why their experience of domestic abuse would not have impacted upon their ability to carry out their sentences at that time.

Skye was 23 and she was serving a sentence for aggravated burglary (non-dwelling) when she was interviewed about her experiences. She had been involved with the CJS for at least two previous offences (although there was limited information available on her record regarding these) but all of her listed offences had taken place during her relationship with her abusive partner. She didn't have any

Gendered Justice? How Women's Attempts to Cope With, Survive,
or Escape Domestic Abuse Can Drive Them into Crime, 75–83
Copyright © 2022 by Jo Roberts
Published under exclusive licence by Emerald Publishing Limited
doi:10.1108/978-1-80262-069-620221010

children and hadn't gained any qualifications at school, but during her time in prison she had completed some courses including hair and beauty and was hoping to do her General Certificate of Secondary Educations (GCSEs). Skye's abusive partner was 13 years older than her and she had been in a relationship with him for a year. During this relationship he had subjected her to serious physical violence but he was also very jealous and controlling and it was his abusive behaviours that Skye said had affected her ability to comply. During Skye's interview she talked about how she had not been reporting to probation which she was required to do as part of her sentence. She explained this was a result of the coercive control and physical abuse she had been subjected to by her partner who monitored her every-day actions, as the quotation which opens this chapter illustrates. Part of her part-ner's controlling behaviour included timing how long it took for Skye to get to and from her probation appointments and she recounted what her abuser would say:

> 'I've been timing you and you've been about 3 hours, 4 hours, it only takes you about an hour to get to probation and back' ... [but] it don't matter where I've gone, do you know what I mean as long as I'm, as long as I'm home I'm alright ... he didn't like that [me going out] whatsoever.

Skye's recollection of her partner's actions demonstrates the extent of con-trol a survivor of domestic abuse can be subjected to and how, for women who are involved in abusive relationships and serving community-based sentences, their abuse can interfere with their ability to serve these sentences. Making the arrangements for Skye's interview also demonstrated the high levels of control she was subjected to (as well as the safety considerations that were central to the planning, and practical implementation, of the study). The interview was conducted at the probation office at the set time Skye would usually meet her probation officer, this was a cautious arrangement to ensure that her partner didn't become aware of her involvement in the study as this could have had seri-ous repercussions for Skye. Due to her abuser timing her outings Skye had to make sure that she left the probation office at the time she would always leave and return home when expected.

For Skye the extent of her abuser's control also stretched further than just timing her journeys to and from probation, he also employed other tactics which disrupted her ability to comply and sometimes prevented her from reporting to probation. As Skye's explanation below demonstrates, her abusive partner would also use her drug addiction as a means of manipulating her and attempting to prevent her from attending probation appointments. As Skye elaborates:

> It was really, really hard, [trying to attend probation] yeah it was, that's why I was breached because I didn't want to come to pro-bation because if I was late, I'd have a slap, so that's why I didn't go to probation, [also] he was saying to me ... 'let's go and pick up gear, let's go and pick up drugs, let's go and pick up this' ...

'I've got appointments to go to love, I can't go pick up drugs and that, you can go pick up the drugs and I can go to my appointments and stuff', no he wouldn't let me do that, whatsoever, he wouldn't let me at all.

As Skye's account highlights, it was as a result of her abusive partner's behaviour that she breached her order and was subsequently sent back to prison. Skye explained that this was due to her abusive partner becoming so controlling and violent towards her after returning from probation accompanied by his attempts to lure her with drugs so she wouldn't attend. Therefore, as a means of preventing these attacks from happening, she stopped attending probation and consequently missed so many appointments that she was breached. Despite the negative consequences this had for Skye, she actually viewed this as an opportunity for her to escape her abusive partner:

because of [ex-partner] … after that [multiple physical assaults after attending probation] then I didn't bother so that was obviously why I was breached, I was going to jail, and I went to prison for 2 months, half of 2 months, I'd do a month [and] … I couldn't wait to go to prison that day.

Initially, for Skye, it was the effects of her abuser's controlling and physically violent behaviour that created a situation whereby she had to choose between attending probation and being assaulted on her return, or simply not attending in order to protect herself from physical violence. Skye's actions to avoid physical abuse combined with her abuser's further manipulation in exploiting her drug addiction which again lured Skye away from her probation appointments therefore culminated in her breaching her order. Consequently, it was the circumstances established and maintained by her abusive partner that led to Skye's further problems with the law.

Skye's circumstances were not uncommon for women serving community-based sentences who were in abusive relationships at the time and one Probation staff member provided another account of a woman that she had supervised who had been unable to attend her probation appointments because of her abusive partner:

she still had to come here [to report to Probation] and her partner didn't want her to come here, so she would fail to attend and she was breached and then had more punishment and then she breached again and then she had a custodial sentence but it wasn't sort of recognised then that, well it's not that she's choosing not to come, it's the fact that she was told she's not allowed to come. Well we can't then say well you take her partner to court, it was the fact that in court, when she was on her own, she was extremely motivated and was telling court she was able to do the sentence,

> but we obviously wanted to get her support and the best way was
> gonna be through the probation, because she had committed this
> offence, but then he wouldn't let her come here and it's like how do
> you deal with that?

(Probation staff member 7)

As this interview extract demonstrates the probation staff member recognised that the woman she was supervising had breached her licence conditions as a consequence of the domestic abuse she was being subjected to. Both Skye's experiences and the Probation staff member's observations demonstrate that some perpetrators of domestic abuse utilise their victim's involvement with the CJS as a further weapon of power and control, in some cases causing their victims further problems with the law. It is important to note, however, that further problems with the law can manifest as a by-product of being subjected to domestic abuse as well as via perpetrators' deliberate interference with their victim's involvement in the CJS.

It was not only Skye who revealed how her experience of domestic abuse had impacted upon her ability to carry out her sentence in the community. For Summer, it was the *deliberate* actions that her abusive ex-husband took, where he actively interfered with her ability to comply with her sentence, that caused her further problems with the CJS. Summer, aged 34, had been convicted of robbery and assault with the intent to rob and this was her first offence. Summer had left school with some GCSEs and had attended college completing a hairdressing course. She had 3 children, 2 with her abusive ex-husband and one with a previous partner. Summer had been sentenced to 24 months custody but at the time of her interview she had recently been released from prison and was now out on licence, being supervised by Probation. Summer disclosed that she had been subjected to domestic abuse within 2 relationships which had lasted nearly 10 years. Summer's first abusive partner was 5 years older than her at the time of their relationship (which started when she was 19 and he was 24) and she described him as very jealous and controlling:

> he used to go out in the mornings, he used to leave the house about
> half past 7, I can't really remember, long time ago, used to lock me
> in the house, he'd come back about 4 or 5, I couldn't go out, then
> it would be like what you been up to? So I had to memorize every-
> thing, what I had done [otherwise I'd get a] lamping.

Not only was Summer's partner extremely controlling he was also physically violent and she recalled how he'd subjected her to severe physical beatings, which included one incident which caused her to lose a baby:

> I was pregnant at the time, I just lost the baby through him beat-
> ing me up, 'cause I hadn't answered the house phone, couldn't
> hear it, obviously there were 2 doors were shut, one being PVC,

white double glazing doors, you can't hear nothing can you? He come in that night kicked me that hard, on the floor, God 'cause he punched me to the floor, kicking me that hard I was peeing with blood, all down my legs, he had to phone an ambulance for me, had to get carried out and that and that was just ... one of many [abusive incidents] with him.

Summer's second relationship was with her ex-husband who had been abusive to her for 7 years. Summer described some of his behaviours:

[...] he was controlling. It was when we split up he used to follow me, threaten every [new] boyfriend, he'd kick the door down one day, while I was in the bed, hit the baby, my newborn at the time, his daughter and I was with a boy, he battered the boy that badly there was blood coming from his eyes, his ears, so I ran downstairs to phone the police, he'd pulled the phone, snapped the phone neat in half, smacked me in the tooth, took off half my tooth. The coppers come there, put a lock on the door and he never got arrested for it.

At the time of her interview Summer described how she had left the relationship with her abusive ex-husband over 6 years ago but he had continued to be abusive towards her after the relationship had ended. At the time of the interview Summer described how her abusive ex-husband was attempting to use her involvement with the CJS as a further mechanism of abuse against her:

I'm on licence, [my abusive ex-husband] is ringing the police saying that ... 'cause I'm with my new partner... he's phoned the coppers saying I'm living up there, I'm out in the pub, I'm doing this, I'm doing that [breaching my licence conditions] ... where I ain't ... he's told CAFCASS, the woman, that he'd be happy if I had nothing to do with the kids now, he got a new wife, he wants a new life and he's trying to get me back to jail.

As Summer had only recently been released from prison any breach of the licence conditions that she had to adhere to would have had a significant impact upon her and her children (whom she was the primary carer of) with one such consequence being recalled to prison. Her ex-husband's actions clearly demonstrate how he was exploiting Summer's vulnerable position (both as a victim of domestic abuse and as a female offender having to comply with a community-based sentence) to continue his abuse towards her as well as reinforce the distinct imbalance of power between them. One of the Probation staff member interviews elaborated upon cases such as Summer's where domestic abuse perpetrators would employ their victim's involvement with the CJS as yet another weapon of abuse:

> [...] they [the abuse perpetrators] hold that string over [the female offenders] by saying I'll send you back to prison, you know, you've got kids ... you won't be able to see your kids when you're back in prison, look what I can do, I've got the power to do it...yeah loads of examples of people just threatening that really to their partners .... (Probation staff member 6)

Circumstances such as those outlined by this probation staff member suggest that the combination of a woman's domestic abuse victimisation as well as her involvement with the CJS compound her vulnerability leading to an increased risk of being further criminalised by the justice system. Therefore, women who are being subjected to domestic abuse whilst attempting to serve their sentences in the community could be perceived as being doubly vulnerable as their abusers can utilise their involvement with the CJS as yet another means of exerting power and control. A woman's status as an offender being exploited by an abuse perpetrator was also identified by Vickers and Wilcox (2011, p. 25) as they found that a woman's 'involvement with the justice system can be an effective means of maintaining power and control over [her]'. This perspective was substantiated by yet another Probation staff member who was interviewed for this research:

> [...] I think in cases of domestic violence, because women are on an order they've got to comply with certain conditions, I think, in a way, they're almost more vulnerable. Particularly if you've got a partner who is very manipulative, they can use that [their sentence/ involvement in the CJS] and use that fear and intimidation and [say] 'if you do this, I'm going to tell probation you were doing this'... (Probation staff member 2)

Both Skye and Summer's accounts were further corroborated by the probation staff member interviews, many of whom identified ways in which a woman's experience of domestic abuse could impact upon her ability to carry out her sentence. For example, these probation staff members recognised a variety of ways that an abuse perpetrator could, either actively or simply as a by-product of perpetrating abuse, affect their victim's ability to comply with orders/ requirements:

> [...] it could be a whole range of things, the [abusive] partner could be literally preventing them from attending [probation appointments] either because they don't want them to attend or they don't want them to leave the house at all. It could be issues of shame whereby the [female offender] doesn't wanna come in and present because they've got injuries or because they don't wanna talk about the issues that are coming up before them. It could just lead to a chaotic lifestyle or other issues that they aren't able to comply, that they aren't able to manage their time effectively, so all sorts

of things really but I think, yeah, it [domestic abuse] can definitely have an impact .... (Probation staff member 15)

There are some women who are told that they're not allowed to come and some women who are too embarrassed to come in, especially if they've been physically assaulted. [It] might be also that they don't have any finances to come in so that they can't afford the bus fare [due to financial abuse] and in all manner of ways. Or what we get is a lot of women who come here with men and the men insist [they attend with their partner] but all the men are now told that no men are allowed in the office on a [women-only reporting day] morning, so quite often when women are in that stifling sort of relationship we've used the women-only reporting to say you have to come in on [women-only reporting day] morning and no men are allowed in the office and then it makes it easier. (Probation Staff Member 9)

As these interview extracts demonstrate there are a wide range of ways that a woman's experience of domestic abuse can impact upon her ability to comply and these findings corroborate the findings of other research. In their study, Vickers and Wilcox (2011) also found that a woman's motivation to attend probation appointments could be affected by her abuser if he was also reporting to probation (for example, where he is serving his own sentence and also attending the same probation office as his victim leading to the woman's reluctance to attend the probation office in case she sees him there). They also identified that some abuse perpetrators would accompany their victims to their probation appointments (something also identified during this study) suggesting that, as just one example, the abusers could be trying to prevent their victims from seeking help for the abuse they are experiencing from probation or any other agencies during their visits to probation. Importantly, Vickers and Wilcox's (2011) work also highlighted that for women experiencing domestic abuse and attempting to serve a sentence in the community, complying with the sentence requirements may not be their primary priority when compared to simply trying to survive the domestic abuse they are being subjected to, which could lead to breach or recall as a consequence. Richie's (1996) study also substantiates this perspective as she recognised that women will often prioritise what is demanded or threatened by an abuser as the risk of not doing so has far greater consequences for the woman (examples include abusers threatening to murder their victims or the victim's children) than the consequences of the CJS. Vickers and Wilcox also pointed to the numbers of women entering custody due to a breach of their community order and the need for the CJS to recognise the context of such breaches, or as they state:

breach of a community order...may on the surface appear to be the result of a lack of personal responsibility [but] the reality is much more complex ... passivity and chaos can be conceptualised as engendered and reinforced by abusive relationships, rather than as the personal responsibility of women offenders. (Vickers and Wilcox, 2011, p. 25)

Identifying ways in which an abuse perpetrator can employ their victim's involvement with the CJS as a further weapon or tool of abuse replicates similar actions taken by perpetrators already recognised as abusive. For example, it is recognised that abusers often threaten to report their victims to other statutory agencies such as social or children's services as a means of controlling them (see Domestic Abuse Intervention Programs, 2011; Hester et al., 2007; Humphreys and Thiara, 2002 and McWilliams and McKiernan, 1993). In the case of this study, however, abuse perpetrators replaced social services with the Probation Service and threatened to report an aspect of their victim's behaviour (which can be actual or indeed fabricated) in order to abuse, punish, or control their victim. In summary, the accounts of the women and probation staff members interviewed for this research demonstrate how an abuser can facilitate or cause their victims further problems with the law in a range of different contexts:

- As part of the abuse inflicted within the abusive relationship.
- As a means of punishing the victim for leaving or attempting to leave the abusive relationship.
- Or as a means of attempting to draw the victim back into the relationship or to continue to maintain control over them.

All of these contexts demonstrate the substantial impact that being subjected to domestic abuse, whether current or after the relationship has ended, can have upon a woman's interaction with the law or the CJS. Importantly, what has been outlined in this chapter suggests there is a need for probation staff to understand the context behind a woman's breach or the behaviours she enacts whilst serving her sentence and this was advocated by one of the Probation staff members interviewed for this study who stated:

> I think Probation, that's one of the things that we're looking at … is the reason why women do breach, and is it because of re-offending? Is it to do with conditions? Then we need as an organisation to look at the conditions we're putting on licences and make sure they are suitable for the woman and … why is somebody not attending? Is it due to childcare? I mean it could be, it could be that if the woman doesn't want to bring the child to the Probation office, which is fair enough, it's not the best environment, she's relying on that partner for childcare and then they don't turn up, potentially then they could breach. (Probation staff member 2)

This interview extract introduces yet another way that an abusive partner could impact upon his victim's ability to comply, by offering to provide childcare and then immediately prior to the woman needing to attend probation failing to do so. Not only does this quotation emphasise the need to better understand the reasons behind why breach occurs (in particular the ways in which a woman's experience of domestic abuse may affect her ability to comply) but also suggests that the woman's circumstances should be taken into account during sentencing. It could be argued that sentencers should ensure that what is being enforced (such as tag or curfew, for example) are appropriate for the woman and cannot be further exploited by an abusive partner.

Chapter 10

Probation Staff Perspectives: The Impact of Women's Domestic Abuse Victimisation Upon Their Sentencing, Support, and Supervision

The primary focus of the study outlined in this book was the women who had been subjected to domestic abuse and who had come into contact with the CJS and the findings which arose from the research are firmly based upon their accounts, perspectives, and words. The interviews with the probation staff, however, also revealed a range of important areas which were not addressed in the women's interviews but make an important contribution to the wider discourses relating to the impact that a woman's experience of domestic abuse can have upon her engagement within the CJS. This chapter will therefore introduce some supplementary matters that were raised by probation staff but focus upon the needs and treatment of women who have experienced domestic abuse who come into contact with the CJS.

All of the probation staff that participated in the research were women, although this was not a deliberate part of the research design. The probation staff occupied a range of different roles but most were Probation Officers (POs) or Probation Service Officers (PSOs) but there was representation from middle management, project based, and research staff. Finally, the length of service of the different staff members ranged from 18 months to 32 years and many had specific responsibilities relating to domestic abuse and/or supervising women.[1]

Pre-Sentence Reports

A pre-sentence report (PSR) is an assessment that is provided to the court by the Probation service which relates to the person that is being sentenced. The PSR

---

[1]For more information about the probation staff who participated in the research see Appendix B – Research Design.

---

doi:10.1108/978-1-80262-069-620221011

contains information relating to the nature and causes of the person's offending, risks the person may pose (and to whom) and also provides possible sentencing options that could be enforced (for further info on PSRs see MOJ, 2021a). PSRs can be provided to the court in two different ways, either orally on the day of sentencing (fast delivery) or the court can request an adjournment before sentencing so that Probation can meet with the person being sentenced to produce a full PSR (full delivery). During the interviews with the probation staff, it was clear how important PSRs are for women coming into contact with the CJS. The importance of PSRs is compounded when the woman's offending has been driven by her experiences of domestic abuse as the PSR process provides one of the only opportunities for her circumstances to be taken into consideration before her sentencing. This probation staff member spoke about the need for PSRs:

> I think they're invaluable especially if the woman feels safe enough in the interview to talk about what has been happening and it can be really difficult to get the information you need because women are ashamed, they're embarrassed about their situation, they don't wanna talk about it, they're still afraid of repercussions, if they tell me something and they're still in that relationship, what am I gonna do about it, am I gonna get social services involved? What's gonna happen to that? … very often we write a pre-sentence report and it's probably the first and only meeting that we're gonna have with that woman and we may only have like an hour/hour and a half to get as much information, so trying to build a relationship with somebody in a really short space of time is difficult … I've met women more than once before writing the pre-sentence report because sometimes it's too difficult to talk about it the first time, they're too upset, so they give you some information but then obviously you need an awful lot more, and sometimes we don't get the interview at all because the woman is just too upset about it, but if you can get a good interview with a woman, she does tell you a lot of information that you can pass on to the court team and you can do some of that in a confidential way, I think the court team, as in barristers, solicitors, the judge, I think if they know a lot of the circumstances that have been going on beforehand it kind of allows them to think outside of just that incident, and that there are all these issues going on in the home, [domestic abuse] is happening, she's terrified of the repercussions. (Probation staff member 13)

As this probation staff member highlights PSRs are invaluable for trying to establish the context of the woman's offending and can provide a time when women are able to disclose their experience of domestic abuse and how this may have affected their involvement in crime. As this probation staff member also outlined there are, however, a range of barriers women face when attempting to disclose domestic abuse victimisation which includes shame, fear of reprisals from the perpetrator, and also fear of intervention from agencies such as social services due to the possible removal of children. As this next probation staff member identifies there are other ways that a woman's experience of domestic abuse can be identified and taken into consideration in sentencing:

> I would like there to be more investigation in regards to ringing the domestic violence unit, ringing social services before sentence because a part of our, we do pre-sentence reports but then there's full reports and then there's fast delivery reports and on our full reports there's, I think there's like 10 sections and one of those sections is relationships, on the fast one relationships are not added. (Probation staff member 7)

There are strong arguments for comprehensive, full-delivery PSRs to be produced for women who are being sentenced given the specific needs of women coming into contact with the CJS, and especially for those women who have been subjected to domestic abuse where this may have driven their involvement in crime. This does not only allow for a better understanding of the circumstances surrounding the woman's offending but also given the implications specific sanctions can have for women who are experiencing domestic abuse when serving their sentences in the community (this will be explored in more detail later in the chapter). Given the prevalence of histories of trauma experienced by women who come into contact with the CJS there is a clear argument for PSRs, both fast and full delivery, to include routine enquiry into whether the woman being sentenced has experienced domestic abuse and how, if at all, her experiences may have contributed to her offending. This interview extract from one of the probation staff member interviews demonstrates why there are calls for routine enquiry into domestic abuse victimisation as part of PSRs:

> [One woman] took … over 50 thousand pounds in benefit fraud over a significant period of time. She was disabled as well and she was just being abused for years and years and years and she had no way of basically financially supporting herself. [Her abusive partner] had a drinking problem as well so all the money would go on his drink and she kind of secretly kept this housing benefit claim up and running over the years to basically make ends meet, but yet she was literally living with no gas and electric and she was disabled … I wrote that report, and the case was put forward and she…got a community order rather than a prison sentence which is what they were looking at, given the amount of money … Yeah there's probably some [other cases where domestic abuse has influenced the woman's offence] driving ones, in the time people fleeing a situation or being quite erratic or emotional after an argument and they've jumped in a car maybe under the influence of alcohol as well, that you now, they hadn't planned on driving but they wanted to just get out of the situation and that was the most important thing to then was to just get out of the situation. (Probation staff member 6)

As this interview extract demonstrates, and as the book as a whole has illustrated, there is a clear need to understand the circumstances behind each woman's offending and the PSRs provide one of the only mechanisms through which this can be investigated to ensure that the context is communicated with the courts.

In recent years there have been calls for the Probation service to adopt a gender-specific approach to PSRs which should include routine enquiry for domestic abuse victimisation, ensuring that questions about whether or not a woman has experienced domestic abuse are asked (see Marougka, 2018 and PRT, 2017a). In their recent briefing the PFT (2017a) also mentioned that a judge they had surveyed would welcome detailed information in PSRs regarding how a woman's experience of domestic abuse may have contributed to her involvement in crime.

Up-Tariffing

Directly linked to the sentencing of women and in particular Chapter 6 and women's accounts of using arrest or imprisonment as a means of escaping domestic abuse and the view that imprisonment can provide women with an escape route or a reprieve from domestic abuse victimisation, interviews with probation staff members revealed further troubling findings. Several probation staff members spoke about how they perceived that, in some cases, magistrates and judges viewed imprisonment as a mechanism through which women who are victims of domestic abuse can access help and suggested that, as a result of such beliefs, the judiciary would sometimes impose custodial sentences specifically to facilitate this. The problem here is that sentencing should reflect the crime committed *not* the support needs of the person being sentenced. The process of allocating women more severe sentences to account for their support needs rather than in response to the actual crime committed, has been labelled 'up-tariffing'.

A number of the probation staff members raised concerns that some magistrates or judges viewed prison as an appropriate, and safe, form of accommodation for female offenders who were victims of domestic abuse, as this probation staff member noted:

> [...] sometimes the court have sent people to prison 'cause they think they'll be safer there, away from their domestic abuse or abusive relationship, but then that has such a big impact on everything else it's not the best thing for them [the woman being sentenced]. (Probation staff member 12)

The view of this probation staff member suggests that this type of up-tariffing is both inappropriate and can have a significant impact on women in the longer term due to being sentenced to custody which can disrupt employment, housing, and childcare. Similarly, sentencers viewing prison as a form of 'respite' for women with chaotic lifestyles, was also identified by Malloch and McIvor (2012) who emphasised the damage that imprisonment can cause women. Malloch and McIvor (2012) assert that for women prisons are places of isolation and violence and when women are imprisoned this can have a significant negative impact on their relationships with their children.

In addition to women being allocated custodial sentences as a form of up-tariffing, Probation staff members also detailed how some magistrates or judges add extra requirements to community-based orders, again, purely as an avenue for women to access support for their domestic abuse victimisation:

> I think sometimes, if the woman presents and she's got quite complex needs, even if the crime isn't that serious they'll be given quite an intensive order, so they'll have a lot to do and it's because OK this woman's got complex needs so we're going to throw everything at them but what you're doing is you're up-tariffing someone. You're giving them a sentence which doesn't fit the crime which they did just because they're perceived as being complex with a lot of needs, it's like, oh well, we'll do this, this and this, and give them a really intensive order and that'll sort everything out and that's not the case. (Probation staff member 2)

> You've also got this idea of up-tariffing that because somebody's got a support need that the only way of getting the support is then giving them probation, a community-based order, but then is that proportionate to what they've done and is that the most appropriate way of dealing with that support need? (Probation staff member 13)

Both of the interview extracts above make comment upon the inappropriateness of allocating women extra requirements in response to their support needs. Although the intention is to requirements the woman with what the sentencers perceive to be much needed support the consequences of being sentenced to custody or being allocated a more complex order can be highly problematic for women and, particularly in the cases of custodial sentences, their children. These consequences not only relate to women's criminal records but also their wider social circumstances in relation to care of children. A recent PRT report (2018) sited research which identified that only a tiny proportion of children remain in their family home when their mothers are sent to prison (the figure included in the report was only 5 percent). The PRT (2018) also noted that for children the other consequences of a mother's imprisonment can also include having to move school or being separated from other family members or siblings. Furthermore, the devastating impact that women being sentenced to custody can have on them in the longer term is highlighted by PRT (2017b). In their briefing the PRT (2017b) highlighted that within one year of leaving prison 48 percent of women are reconvicted. The percentage of women reconvicted within one year of release from prison significantly increases to a 61 percent reconviction rate when the woman has served a sentence of less than 12 months.

Another probation staff member interview also suggested that when women are up-tariffed, seemingly for their own good, they can subsequently encounter further problems with the law if they are unable to comply with what they have been asked to do:

> how far should somebody's personal circumstances or victimisation be taken into account in terms of what sentence they're given and the severity of the sentence? ... somebody could be potentially up-tariffed for their own good, or given criminal justice interventions which are intended to be helpful and supportive but actually can then sometimes end up with them [the offenders] breaching and ending up in prison which is not helpful ... so I think it's a really complex area. (Probation staff member 15)

Therefore, although it is helpful that magistrates and judges recognise the specific support needs of women involved with the CJS, it was felt that up-tariffing is not an appropriate solution for women to gain access to the support they need, as this Probation staff member elaborated:

> [...] [the courts] see a woman come before them with a multitude of issues who's in complete chaos and they think prison is a way of helping her sort that out, which sometimes is for a short-term thing but...that's not what it's there for ....(Probation staff member 15)

One of the probation staff also compared the way men and women are sentenced, suggesting that due to their complex needs women are more likely to be up-tariffed or, in other words, be allocated a more severe punishment:

> I think the difficulty is, if you've got a woman who's only committed an offence of criminal damage but then they've got all of these needs, and you almost think you need to address all of these so they don't commit an offence again but a male who's committing criminal damage might just get a fine, so is it fair that that women has to then become part of this system?. (Probation staff member 11)

The process of 'up-tariffing' female offenders has been identified within other studies, including within research completed by Barry and McIvor (2010, p. 34) who noted that:

> Balancing a woman's needs for assistance and support against the risk of up-tariffing them was reported to represent a constant dilemma for practitioners in the absence of alternative 'welfare-oriented' disposals.

Therefore, these findings suggest that the CJS can further punish women who have experienced domestic abuse by allocating more severe sentences which account for support needs rather than reflect the crimes committed. In addition, the practice of up-tariffing suggests that sentencers may be unaware of the impact certain court disposals have on the women being sentenced, and in many cases their children, but also suggests that non CJS-based disposals should be available where being provided with the support needed does not disadvantage the woman in reference to her criminal record.

Hedderman and Barnes (2015) discussed the problematic outcomes of up-tariffing in their work on the sentencing of women. They noted that whilst in many cases the sentencer's intention may be to help the woman before them the reality is that a sentence of increased severity can further stigmatise a woman and add to her criminal record. They also noted that up-tariffing can put women at increased risk of custody. This can transpire either due to the women's chaotic lives which result in them being unable to comply with their sentences where they could subsequently be breached. This could also be resultant from missing out earlier steps in the sentencing tariff meaning that the women then '... have less distance to travel before "running out of road" if they reoffend and [then find] themselves at risk of custody' (Hedderman and Barnes, 2015, p. 17).

Conclusively, the process of up-tariffing suggests that the CJS may further victimise women who have experienced domestic abuse by sentencing them to sanctions which reflect their support needs rather than the crimes they have committed. Interestingly, this also suggests that a woman's experience of domestic abuse may not only impact upon her involvement in crime but also upon her sentencing in terms of the severity of punishment she receives for her actions.

The Impact of Particular Court Disposals/Sanctions for Women Who are Being Subjected to Domestic Abuse

Another area of concern arising from the interviews with probation staff members included the impact that particular sanctions can have for women who are being subjected to domestic abuse where the sanctions themselves can put women at risk or cause them to encounter further problems with the law. Curfew, where women are confined at home for a certain number of hours, was deemed to be particularly problematic and dangerous for women experiencing domestic abuse:

> one example is they don't feel they can exit the relationship because they've got the curfew and that would breach their curfew but also it means even if they're not living with the person, the person knows exactly when they've gotta be in, so they can target them that way. There's so many different ways that it's just so inappropriate, so I'd almost like to see as a kind of general rule no curfews for females unless you can argue why in this case you're very, very, very, very confident that this person's not gonna have any kind of harm implications as a result of you proposing it, 'cause there [are] other options out there. (Probation staff member 6)

As this probation staff member account demonstrates, the consequences of curfew could cause women to feel trapped in an abusive relationship with no route of escape. In addition, this probation staff member also suggests that in cases where the women are not living with their abusive partner, the perpetrators of abuse may still have knowledge of the licence conditions or order requirements and be aware that the women are confined to the house for a certain period of time. This can be extremely dangerous as abuse perpetrators could choose this particular time to target their victims, or indeed their children, knowing that she is unable to escape, or, leave the house to come after the children if he chooses to take them or encourage them to misbehave. Circumstances like this therefore also provide further opportunities for abuse perpetrators to exploit their victims' vulnerability by interfering with their conditions or requirements, something which has unconsciously been made possible by the CJS. As this second interview extract demonstrates curfew can therefore cause women subjected to domestic abuse to encounter further problems with the law if they make any attempt to escape the relationship whilst under curfew as they would be breaching their requirements or conditions:

> in terms of things like curfews [and] tagging ... if they're [the woman is] in an abusive relationship and they're tagged to an address they can't get out, they can't leave, or they could be in more trouble if they do, so it's about being mindful I suppose of those things ... but it's just having the foresight to see that there potentially could be something going on for her at home ... especially things like licence conditions and terms of curfews, I'd be very much mindful and afraid to put curfews on [female offenders]. (Probation staff member 13)

As both of these Probation staff member interview extracts illustrate when sentencing women, it is important to have an understanding of whether the woman is in an abusive relationship as being sentenced to curfew or tag can have highly problematic consequences for women both in relation to their safety and possible further criminalisation. Importantly, however, some actions can be taken to prevent situations such as these, as another probation staff member interview suggested:

> curfews are usually 7pm to 7am and one of the things that we check with the domestic abuse unit is that there's been no police call outs to that address involving those people and that would be, whether it's a victim or a perpetrator, so that would be really important. (Probation staff member 9)

The probation staff member interviews also raised the need to recognise the impact of financial abuse and how imposing fines on women who are subject to domestic abuse can also cause further problems for them, as this probation staff member explains:

Things like financial abuse [and] imposing massive fines on people is gonna have a massive impact on their non-existent financial
situation, the situation they're in already, but also the stress and
arguments that it may cause if there's, on-going things [such as] if
they don't pay bailiffs [they] could come to the property, that could
be another thing that could escalate in [regards to] the violence
that she's experiencing. (Probation staff member 13)

Elaborating upon the problem of fines for women who are subjected to domestic abuse this probation staff member also mentioned the need to look at the patterns of women's offending to better understand what could be driving it, which
in the case she details appears to be financial abuse. The probation staff member
elaborates on one case where, as a result of the imposition of fines, one woman
was placed in a problematic situation which saw her returning to court the consequences of which led to an extended criminal record:

[…] in terms of things like domestic abuse, the financial side of it
… I'd seen this woman in court … she'd been in court … I'd seen
her about 2 or 3 times [in 6 months], the first time that I'd seen her
it was something to do with benefit fraud, quite low level amount
of money, and so she was dealt with by a community penalty not
linked to probation, I think it was a fine and then I'd seen her maybe
a couple of months later and she'd stolen a chicken and other bits
and pieces from a supermarket … but she was dealt with on both
occasions by community penalties, fines, and then she came in the
third time for something similar, low level shoplifting or theft and
she'd highlighted to her solicitor at this point that she was in significant debt and obviously the impact of the fines and things that
she'd got from the courts previously were having an impact on how
she was managing her debt and it was only at that point that they
thought, hang on, let's get the probation service involved and at
that point we didn't do a pre-sentence report, it was an oral report
meeting, and it was almost like a relief to her that she could sit and
speak to someone and I was involved in the interview at that point.
She'd been offending for, probably over a year's pattern, she was
in a violent relationship and these offences happened in quick suc-
cession during this relationship, no previous convictions, probably
highly unlikely to be involved in the criminal justice system if she
wasn't in this relationship. (Probation staff member 13)

The situation described by this probation staff member, although she does not
explicitly state so, suggests that this particular woman became involved in crime
as a result of financial abuse as she was unable to afford basic necessities such
as food. Given that all the offences outlined in this case were financially motivated and she was being subjected to domestic abuse it is highly possible that her
offending was a consequence of financial abuse. In this situation, it is clear to see

that the allocation of fines only exacerbated her financial problems and led the victim of domestic abuse to encounter further problems with the law.

During the study there were more direct references to women committing crimes due to financial abuse including:

> [financial abuse] got them involved in the criminal justice system, I'm just thinking of specific cases now where some females have been so worried that there's no food in the cupboards that they've gone out to shoplift for fear of not having that dinner on the table when the partner returns from the pub. (Probation staff member 7)

> [The abusive] relationship becomes a major part of [their life] so you get shoplifters because they're got no access to funds ... I think certainly people who've got no control over their finances or have very limited money because their partners are either controlling that or they're spending all their money on their partners. A lot of the time it's stuff for their children [that they are shoplifting] it's not shiny stuff it's food or it's clothing for the children, it's what they'd class as essentials. (Probation staff member 3)

Women committing crimes which are resultant from the financial abuse they are subjected to was also something identified by Moe (2004). One of the pathways that Moe established related to women's financial survival and referred to women committing crimes due to economic necessity in order to survive or flee their abusive relationships. In cases such as these, where women's crimes are clearly financially motivated and could be the result of economic abuse it is imperative that courts do not then enforce sanctions that further victimise them or make it impossible for them to comply with their sentence.

As all of the above interview extracts demonstrate certain sanctions can have particularly problematic consequences for women who are being subjected to domestic abuse and are carrying out their sentences in the community. Therefore, in order to prevent abusers being able to exploit their victims' further vulnerability, resultant from their involvement in the CJS, or possibly facilitate their further punishment, it could be argued that sentencers should consider the appropriateness and safety implications of the types of orders/requirements allocated to women. Not only should sentencers be better equipped with knowledge regarding how a woman's experience of domestic abuse can impact upon her pathway into crime they should also be mindful of the impact that certain sentencing decisions can have upon a woman's ability to comply with their orders as well as the wider impact that the sentences can have upon the women's lives (and where applicable, their children's lives). One of the recommendations made by the PRT (2017a) in their report addressing how domestic abuse can function as a driver to women's offending is for the Sentencing Council to ensure those delivering sentences acknowledge and take into consideration how particular sentences can affect women who have been subjected to domestic abuse, in particular the impact of imprisonment on both women and their children.

Women-Only Reporting Days/Times and Options for Court Mandated Requirements/Conditions

During the interviews with probation staff members there were discussions about elements of good practice and processes which were already in place, or being introduced, which sought to address some of the issues raised earlier in this book including women's ability to comply with their community-based sentences when experiencing domestic abuse (as outlined in Chapter 9). At the time of the research the Wales Probation Trust had already started to implement targeted processes to help address some of the issues that women who come into contact with the CJS and who are being subjected to domestic abuse can face. One such example of a process to address some of the barriers to women's compliance was the introduction of women-only reporting days/times. The women-only reporting days/times were specifically allocated days/times when men would not be allowed onto the probation office premises and these days/times were identified as being specifically helpful to women experiencing domestic abuse. As this probation staff member noted the process of women-only reporting removes some of the problems that attending the same environment as men brings (which could mean being accompanied by or coming into contact with an abusive partner or ex-partner):

> In terms of coming into probation...in the past women have turned up to appointments with the male perpetrator and they need them to come into the appointment with them and when you ask the male to leave you see this change in behaviour, the change in how the [women] then respond to you, but it's a way of them still being controlled isn't it. (Probation staff member 13)

Not only does women-only reporting, therefore, remove the opportunity for abuse perpetrators to accompany their victim to their probation appointments it also addresses the often male-dominated environment that probation offices can be which can be particularly intimidating for women who have been subjected to domestic abuse:

> We've already set up women-only reporting times so that women who are suffering domestic abuse don't have to come in and sit in a room potentially with people they may not feel comfortable with ... the next step to that would be not having [women reporting to probation] in the same building at all, but having it in more of a female-centred environment which is something we'll be looking at possibilities for. So those are some basic things that could help with compliance, but it might be much more complex than that, it might be to do with power and control, somebody's actually not letting them come in or ... things are just too chaotic in their lives for them to be able to comply ... it's about the understanding and the professionalism of the practitioner really to know who they're

working with, to understand them, to use their professional judge-
ment and to work with that case as best as they can to deal with
the issues but, it's not easy. (Probation staff member 15)

As this probation staff member suggests introducing restrictions where only
women can report on particular days or at particular times provides a space that
may be less traumatising for women to report in, particularly if they are experiencing or have experienced domestic abuse. Not only can this provide a more
appropriate environment for women who come into contact with the CJS but
the process of women-only reporting may help to address compliance issues by
removing some of the barriers women face in attending probation appointments.
Although, as this staff member recognises, compliance in cases where women are
experiencing domestic abuse can be more complex and women-only reporting
cannot remove all barriers women experiencing domestic abuse face.

A further facet of women-only reporting that may be beneficial for women
being subjected to domestic abuse is the provision of other support services which
are provided by agencies external to probation. Therefore, in addition to women-
only reporting times providing women with a less intimidating atmosphere these
sessions also allow women to access other support services without any interference from male partners as this probation staff member outlines:

> [Women-only reporting] gives women the opportunity to come to
> a reporting centre [when] they know there's not gonna be males
> there ... the bigger picture is that women are given an opportu-
> nity to come to a service that's there specifically for them and that
> there's support services besides probation offered to them which
> they can use or not use if they want to. If they want some advice
> it's there for them and we're hoping in the future that we're gonna
> be able to have things like New Pathways, a counselling service and
> things here for women as well, 'cause that can be really difficult
> thing [for them] to access ....(Probation staff member 13)

As this probation staff member details, during women-only reporting sessions
the Wales Probation Trust also arranged for additional services including sexual assault services (New Pathways), counselling services, drug/alcohol services,
domestic abuse services, and child-care facilities to be available to women as a
means of supporting them to access the support they may require. As has been
identified throughout the book many of the women who come into contact with
the CJS, and especially those being subjected to domestic abuse, have extremely
chaotic lives, and therefore bringing a wide range of services together in one single space can provide them with a much-needed opportunity to access support
which, if they had to travel to each organisation individually, they may not be
able to access. Not only can this help support the women but the provision of
support from other services may also help tackle compliance issues by addressing other criminogenic factors (such as financial difficulties, employment, and
drug or alcohol use – all of which can be connected to women being subjected to

domestic abuse). The process of women-only reporting also aligns with a more trauma-informed and gender-responsive approach to the supervision of women who come into contact with the CJS as it acknowledges the impact victimisation can have upon women's engagement with probation.

It should of course be mentioned that outside of probation there are other existing provisions for women who come into contact with the CJS that are women-only, employ trauma-informed approaches and attempt to address the complex and interlinked issues faced by the women who access them. An example of this would be Women's Community Services (WCSs), also known as integrated women offender services, which often operate as a one-stop shop service where both statutory and voluntary, specialist charities and criminal justice organisations work together. The diverse range of WCSs play a key part in supporting women who are at risk of offending, can be used to divert women away from the CJS and contribute to women's desistance from crime. A range of work has attested to the benefits of such services (Radcliffe et al., 2013; Corston, 2007; Gelsthorpe et al., 2007) which are described as 'holistic' and which focus on women's often complex needs which can drive their offending and contribute to their ability to desist from crime (including women's experience of domestic abuse). In her report Corston (2007) identified WCSs as an example of good practice and suggested they should be expanded across England and Wales. Therefore, although the Wales Probation Trust had developed some processes which may better support women serving sentences in the community and address some of the barriers associated with completing community-based sentences, these women may be better supported in a different environment, such as a WCS.

Training Needs of Criminal Justice Practitioners

The interviews with probation staff members also suggested that advanced training on domestic abuse, specifically relating to the ways in which women's experiences of domestic abuse may drive their offending, disrupt their ability to comply with their sentences and interfere with desistance, may be incredibly beneficial for a range of CJS practitioners including those who sentence as well as those who supervise and support women engaged with the CJS.[2] Multiple probation staff members mentioned the need for further training, including this probation staff member who noted that although training was already provided for staff supervising offenders who *perpetrate* abuse, there was an absence of training regarding

---

[2]Just to note that given that the study outlined in this book was completed in 2015, there may have been significant developments in regard to the training received by those working in Probation which may already address these areas. It is important, however, to include this section as it demonstrates the need for such training and that probation staff themselves have recognised both the need for, and benefits of, specialist training on how a woman's experience of domestic abuse can impact on women who come into contact with the CJS.

how to better support women coming into contact with the CJS who have been *subjected* to domestic abuse:

> We do training on domestic abuse and we're offered training … more linked towards the male perpetrator and how we manage them within the service, how we challenge their beliefs, we look at their offences, what they've committed, the things that they've done to their partner [and] how we challenge that and manage their risks in the community … the training's there for that but I don't think the training is very often there for us to think about the female [victim], the things that she may have been going through. [We should] ask questions about when did the relationship start, how is the relationship, what's home life like for you? It's things like checking for [domestic abuse related] call-outs and things like that, where there may not be any but it's about exploring feelings and I suppose it's building a relationship with that female isn't it? And allowing her to feel like she can trust you to tell you about the relationship that she's been through … giving her the perspective that she's not on her own, that there's lots of other women that are in her position and that she doesn't need to be embarrassed or ashamed by the situation that she's in 'cause it's not actually her that's doing it. (Probation staff member 13)

As the above quotation suggests, and the wider content of this book corroborates, it is imperative that probation staff members who are supervising women are aware of the women's home lives and their significant relationships as these can have a substantial impact upon their pathways into crime, their ability to carry out their sentence, and their pathways out of crime. This staff member further elaborates on the importance of recognising how a woman's relationship can impact upon her involvement in crime:

> I think there's more training needed, especially victim-related [as] for a long time within probation particularly, the victim work is completed by the victim's officer and we as probation officers are dealing with the risk and I think there needs to be a bit more of the two hats going on really. I think that definitely needs to change in the future, that we need to think more about our offenders being victims and not just the offence they've committed. As I've said before, lots of female offending is linked to their relationship, if they haven't got money to feed their children they're gonna go shoplifting, they're going to commit a theft because they've got responsibilities and they've got a duty to protect their children and that far outweighs the legal system then, and that could happen, time and time again and probably will if they're not out of that relationship …. (Probation staff member 13)

It could be argued that better equipping probation staff with an understanding of how a woman's domestic abuse victimisation can impact her offending would not only lead to better support for the woman who has come into contact with the CJS but could also affect better compliance and desistence, therefore, acting as a mutually beneficial process.

One of the probation staff members interviewed suggested that any training provided to CJ practitioners relating to the impact of domestic abuse should be provided by experts working in the field of domestic abuse:

> I was a volunteer for Victim Support so I had a lot of training working with victims of crime and I had specific training on working with victims of domestic violence, working with victims of sexual violence, working with vulnerable and intimidated witnesses …. I was quite lucky that I had a knowledge and understanding of issues of victimisation, which can apply to women [offenders] and I think sometimes particularly as a practitioner within the Trust you get a lot of experience of working and dealing with perpetrators of domestic violence and the issues specifically related to perpetrators but you may not get the training on dealing with victimisation …. I think that's really, really important when you're working with women offenders to always bear that in mind. I think you need domestic abuse agencies who've got really good knowledge and understanding of that area, to actually come in and deliver sessions to staff or work with probation on writing a programme for staff and that then being delivered. (Probation staff member 2)

This is a vital standpoint as those working with survivors of domestic abuse will have an expert understanding of the impact that domestic abuse can have on women's lives and are therefore best placed to provide training on the wide range of impacts of domestic abuse.[3]

As this probation staff member also notes, it is not only probation staff that would benefit from domestic abuse training, but given the issues outlined earlier in this chapter such as up-tariffing and the impact of particular sanctions for women who are being subjected to domestic abuse, sentencers may also benefit from a better understanding of the impact of domestic abuse on women's pathways into crime:

---

[3]I was invited by HMPPS, specifically their Effective Practice and Service Improvement Group, to produce a 7-minute briefing on how domestic abuse can function as a driver to women's offending which has contributed to a small element of their training and understanding of how domestic abuse can impact upon a woman's pathway into crime as well as her ability to comply with her sentence. This briefing has been distributed to all staff working for HMPPS in England and Wales (Roberts and HMPPS Effective Practice and Service Improvement Group, 2020).

I'd love to do some training of magistrates that would be a really powerful way of making them understand [the implications of sentences]. I'd love to be able to give them some real case examples ... I've got one recently where they just sentenced somebody and remanded her in custody and the implications now for her it's just been so huge and I'd love to just sit there and say your decision on that day has now caused this person to end up back in an abusive relationship, into sex working ... I would like to see sentencers have some [training] ... you've got specific DV courts, where they deal with the perpetrators, maybe even having a specific court where the chair of the magistrates, the lead magistrate, has been trained in issues to do with female offenders and trauma and domestic abuse and sexual violence, so at least then [they] ... could then advise the 2 other people on the bench accordingly ... and have a specific female court. I'd quite like to see ... a dedicated report writer for female offenders [who] would have the understanding of the complexity of their needs as well. (Probation staff member 6)

As both the interview extract above and this book as a whole have demonstrated there are a wide range of ways in which a woman's domestic abuse victimisation can contribute to her involvement in crime, her sentencing, her ability to comply with her sentence, and her ability to desist from offending. As a consequence, it is imperative that professionals working in the CJS are provided with the necessary information about how the various criminal justice processes can further victimise women who have been subjected to domestic abuse. Therefore, training would be beneficial to individuals working in a wide range of criminal justice roles including Magistrates, Judges, wider CPS staff, and the Police service. It is not just a recommendation arising from this study for training on the links between a woman's experience of domestic abuse and her pathway into crime to be available to criminal justice professionals; this is also a call made by the PRT (2017a). In their recent report, which explores how domestic abuse victimisation can function as a driver to women's offending, the PRT (2017a) suggest that the Police service, CPS and HMPPS should all receive specific training in this area.

Drawing upon the outcomes of this study I would suggest that training for CJS professionals to better support women who come into contact with the CJS should address the following areas:

- Awareness raising: understanding the whole range of abusive behaviours that constitute domestic abuse and coercive control.
- How domestic abuse victimisation can impact upon women's pathways into crime.
- How a woman's experience of domestic abuse can impact upon her ability to comply with a community-based sentence.
- How a woman's experience of domestic abuse can impact on desistence.

Chapter 11

Conclusions, Recommendations and Implications

Before summarising the conclusions drawn from the study outlined in this book it is important to state that the research did not seek to prove a causal relationship between a woman's experience of domestic abuse and her involvement in crime. Given the complexities of the women's lives and circumstances surrounding their involvement in crime a reductionist, mono-causal explanation where domestic abuse is identified as the *solitary* contributing factor should not be applied. Given the significant prevalence of domestic abuse experienced by women who have come into contact with the CJS it is, however, imperative to explore and attempt to understand how this commonly occurring experience may affect women's behaviour and actions, particularly their pathways into crime.

Moreover, neither did the study seek to absolve women of any responsibility for the crimes they committed but it is perhaps important to reflect upon Dworkin's (1993) suggestion that women who have experienced domestic abuse and who have committed crime are not innocent of their crimes, but their behaviour instead reflects the actions they had to take to survive, the consequences of which brought them into conflict with the law. Lastly, the purpose of the research was not to develop a generalisable theory of women's pathways into crime which is applicable to all women who have come into contact with the CJS. Instead, the study facilitated an in-depth and qualitative exploration of, and an insight into, the complex relationship between women's experiences of domestic abuse and their pathways into crime.

Other Factors Which Can Contribute to Women's Pathways into Crime

There is a need to recognise that many of the women who were interviewed for this study, as well as the wider population of women who come into contact with the CJS, have often experienced *multiple* forms of victimisation or trauma. Some of the women involved in this study had also been subjected to abuse during

Gendered Justice? How Women's Attempts to Cope With, Survive, or Escape Domestic Abuse Can Drive Them into Crime, 101–113
Copyright © 2022 by Jo Roberts
Published under exclusive licence by Emerald Publishing Limited
doi:10.1108/978-1-80262-069-620221012

childhood (this included being sexually or domestically abused[1]), had been victims of rape and sexual assault as adults, had been subjected to other forms of violence perpetrated by men who were not their intimate partners and many had experienced other forms of trauma such as bereavement or the loss of the custody of their children (where the latter was often a result of their domestic abuse victimisation). It should be noted that this research focussed solely on women's domestic abuse victimisation and, as a result, did not explore any of the aforementioned forms of trauma or victimisation and how these may impact upon the women's pathways into crime. As a result, it should be acknowledged that other forms of victimisation or trauma may have also impacted upon, or contributed to, the women's involvement in crime. How the intersections and culmination of women's multiple forms of victimisation may impact on their pathways into crime would be an area that may benefit from further research.

It is also important to state that other factors *outside* of a woman's experience of victimisation and trauma could have either alternatively, or additionally, impacted upon how she came into contact with the CJS. For example, the group of women involved in this study were also characterised by a range of other factors that can contribute to involvement in crime. These additional factors, which have been identified as criminogenic, included lack of formal education, experience of poverty or financial difficulty, substance use, mental health problems, and a pre-existing history of offending (MOJ, 2012b; 2013c; Department of Justice, 2010). It is, however, important to recognise the correlation that exists between a woman's experience of domestic abuse and many of the criminogenic factors mentioned above such as substance use, mental health problems and financial difficulties as many of these can be introduced, exploited, or exacerbated by perpetrators of domestic abuse.

For many of the women involved in the study their lives were both chaotic and complicated, yet what was consistent was the pivotal effect that being subjected to domestic abuse had upon their actions, behaviours, and life choices. The women's experiences and perspectives therefore corroborate Maloney et al.'s (2009, p. 429) statement, which although it references women in custody it can also be applied to women serving community-based sentences:

> trauma is intricately linked both directly and indirectly to the
> female criminal pathway. Indeed, trauma is correlated with men-
> tal and physical illness and dysfunction, maladaptive high risk

---

[1]During their interviews some of the women described their childhood memories which included recollections of their mothers being subjected to domestic abuse. I do not use the term 'witnessing' domestic abuse for children who grow up in households where domestic abuse is being perpetrated because I believe that children are also victims in their own right as they do not simply observe the abuse taking place, they are directly affected by it and are often the target of the abuse as well as the perpetrator's partner.

behaviours and socio-economic disadvantage which characterise imprisoned women.

It is also vital to state that not all women who have been subjected to domestic abuse will become involved in crime, however, women from that demographic were not included in this study. As a result, it was not possible to explore or identify types of coping mechanisms that women employ which may have positive outcomes for them or, alternatively, may divert them away from involvement in crime.

Concluding Comments

As outlined in this book, women's experiences of domestic abuse or coercive and controlling relationships can contribute to their pathways into crime. Yet despite a wide range of literature testifying to the existence of a relationship between a woman's experience of domestic abuse and her involvement in crime, prior to this research there had been very little in-depth, qualitative exploration of how this relationship may operate, specifically in relation to the under-researched demographic of women serving community-based sentences. Therefore, the study outlined in this book expands upon the findings of existing research (Ferraro, 2006; Jones, 2008; Moe, 2004; Comack, 2000; Richie, 1996) and provides an important contribution to international literature.

In contrast to existing studies which have predominantly focussed upon the minority demographic of women in prison this study explored the experiences of women who were serving their sentences in the community. As a result, the research enabled examination of ways in which a woman's experience of domestic abuse victimisation may impact upon more common types of crime and those which better reflect women's general patterns of offending. Furthermore, the study exposed ways in which a woman's experience of domestic abuse could influence her behaviours and actions in both an immediate and longer-term context highlighting a much broader set of circumstances in which domestic abuse victimisation can impact upon women's pathways into crime.

The study expanded upon already existing understandings of the ways in which a woman's experience of domestic abuse can cause her to come into conflict with the law, and determined that women's pathways into crime can be far better understood when contextualised by their domestic abuse victimisation. By focussing upon the interaction between domestic abuse perpetrator and victim and exploring the ways in which women cope with, resist, and respond to the domestic abuse they are subjected to this study identified a range of ways in which women's experiences of domestic abuse can contribute to their pathways into crime. The principle conclusion which arose from the research is that the relationship between a woman's experience of domestic abuse and her involvement in crime extends far further than women simply offending *with*, *against* or *on behalf of* their abuse perpetrator. Instead, the study revealed that women who have been subjected to domestic abuse can commit crime: *without their abuser being present, after they have exited an abusive relationship* or *many years after the abuse has ended*, yet their actions can still be *attributed to their experience of domestic abuse*. Consequently, the research provides evidence of a diverse and complex relationship between a woman's domestic abuse victimisation and her involvement in crime which captures how a woman's pathway into crime, or indeed her criminalisation, can manifest as a *by-product* of her attempts to *cope with, survive, or escape* domestic abuse.

The findings of the study therefore demonstrate how a broader approach should be taken when attempting to understand how women's domestic abuse victimisation can impact on their pathways into crime. Such approaches should recognise how women's behaviours and actions can be influenced either directly or indirectly or, alternatively, result from actions taken in the immediate or longer term as a response to their domestic abuse victimisation. Notably, this research exposed the long-term effect that a woman's experience of domestic abuse can have on her behaviour and actions which can be enacted outside of her abusive relationship or situation. Therefore, the study demonstrated that women's experiences of domestic abuse can affect their immediate behaviours as well as actions taken in the longer term where those actions are affected and contoured by their historical or previous experiences of domestic abuse. The findings of the research therefore suggest that the coping mechanisms women employ in response to the abuse they experience are part of an on-going, long-term process which can be triggered at a range of different points in their lives. As a result these coping mechanisms, attributed to the domestic abuse they have experienced but which can affect them across their life span, should also be taken into consideration to contextualise their involvement in crime.

The findings of the study also impart a form of social commentary upon how the lack of adequate support or protection afforded to victims of domestic abuse, specifically by criminal justice agencies, can contribute to women's pathways into crime (or compound the desperate circumstances women find themselves in). As has been demonstrated the types of coping mechanisms women can employ are often reliant upon the availability of, and access to, resources to help them (see also Kelly, 1988). Consequently, when there is an absence of support or lack of safe routes women can use to remove themselves from abusive relationships they may turn to crime, and more specifically crime severe enough to lead to imprisonment, as a means of escape or reprieve. Actions such as this may also represent a '... cry for help ...' (Probation staff member 6) and consequently demonstrates the pivotal impact that domestic abuse can have upon a woman's life, behaviour and, for some, their pathways into crime.

One of the most significant outcomes of the study was its demonstration of how perpetrators of domestic abuse can employ the CJS itself as an additional weapon of abuse whether enacted as a means of forcing the woman back into the relationship or punishing her for leaving it. Moreover, the study also provided examples of how perpetrators of domestic abuse actively interfere with their victim's ability to comply with their sentences which can lead to women's further problems with the law. Both of these discoveries illustrate how women who are subjected to domestic abuse and involved with the CJS as an offender are doubly vulnerable.

Lastly, but in conjunction with women's increased vulnerability, the study also documented how criminal justice responses to women's offending can criminalise, re-victimise, and re-traumatise already vulnerable women. This was evidenced by sentencing decisions, and in particular the practice of up-tariffing where women are allocated sentences on the basis of their domestic abuse support needs as opposed to the actual crime that has been committed. When the sentences women are given are more severe or where they are sentenced to imprisonment to access support this will have a long-term impact on women, and in many cases their children. As Roberts and Townhead (2015, p. 6) highlight: 'There is significant need amongst women in the criminal justice system … [yet] criminal justice responses [can] reinforce women's experiences of powerlessness and subjugation, causing further harm'. Therefore, the implications of this research stretch far wider than the CJS alone and demonstrate a need to holistically approach domestic abuse not only to address women's offending and re-offending, but, perhaps most importantly, the prevention of further harm to women themselves.

Recommendations Arising from the Study

Further Research

Although the study outlined in this book was preliminary, and the connection between a woman's experience of domestic abuse and her involvement in crime cannot be proven to be causal, the tentative links identified demonstrate a range of ways that this connection can manifest and that is worthy of further research. Whilst undertaking the research the complexities and diversity of the relationship between women's experiences of domestic abuse and their pathways into crime became increasingly apparent and there is still much to learn about how this relationship operates. This is of particular necessity for women completing community-based sentences as prior to this study, and despite the fact that these women are much more widely representative of women who come into contact with the CJS, they are a demographic that has hitherto been omitted from analysis. It is once again worth stating that the female prison population represents a tiny minority of women who come into contact with the CJS and as a result it is imperative that we continue to better understand the gendered pathways that women follow, or perhaps a more appropriate description would be: are forced to follow, into crime. Moreover, as this book has demonstrated, a woman's experience of domestic abuse does not only impact upon her journey into the CJS it can also have consequences for her continued involvement in or departure out of it, as the chapter on women's compliance signified. If the desire is, rightly-so, to prevent women from ever entering the CJS we must endeavour to develop a broader understanding of the gendered pathways women follow and how to divert women away from the CJS, responding with appropriate support instead of punishment.

Unfortunately, the research outlined in this book was exploratory and the limitations associated with completing doctoral research, namely time and capacity, did not allow for a larger number of women to participate in the study but there are so many voices left to hear. As a result, a key recommendation arising from this study is for more research to be undertaken to continue to develop an understanding of how a woman's experience of domestic abuse can contribute to her involvement in crime. Therefore, the research conducted could be replicated in other geographical regions of the UK or indeed internationally.

A further vital recommendation arising from this research derives from the lack of an ethnically diverse sample. The ethnically homogenous sample was not a deliberate choice but this could reflect the lack of diversity of the women being supervised by the Wales Probation Trust, my ethnicity as a researcher (white British), or a myriad of other barriers that women from black and minoritised communities may face when deciding about whether they want, or are able, to participate in research.[2] Consequently, there is a clear need to complete further research with black and minoritised women who come from a wide range of communities in order to develop a comprehensive and inclusive understanding of the diverse ways in which a woman's experience of domestic abuse can impact upon her pathway into crime.

Better Understanding of the Overlap Between Victimisation and Offending

Rumgay (2004) notes that the CJS relies heavily upon the binary categories of victim and offender and when faced with women who present dual identities as both this creates an obstacle for the development of policy and practice in the field of criminal justice as it poses problems for culpability and allocation of punishment.

The findings of the study suggest that there is a need to reject the binary identification of women as either victim or offender which is often thrust upon them when they come into contact with the CJS. By better acknowledging and addressing the overlap between these two polarised identities and recognising the relationship that exists between women's victimisation and their involvement in crime we can start to view women who come into contact with the CJS how they should be viewed: as human beings that are often in need of support not punishment. This is a perspective shared by one of the probation staff members who explained:

> I think it's just important to keep in mind when you're dealing with someone and they have committed that offence, about their own experience of victimisation as well. That even though they're there as an offender and they've committed an offence to take a holistic approach and look at their background as well. (Probation staff member 2)

---

[2]Examples of barriers could include language barriers, or, as all women who participated in the research had to identify themselves as having experienced domestic abuse the specific forms of abuse that women from black and minoritised groups might experience, such as so-called honour-based violence where a woman's extended family could be involved in the abuse, could make it incredibly difficult for them to safely participate in research.

Given the documented widespread trauma and victimisation that women who come into contact with the CJS have experienced and the implications this can have for their pathways into crime this should be further explored to improve understandings of the causes of, and motivations behind, women's involvement in crime, and more importantly to address women's needs to prevent them from being subjected to further harm. In addition, it is imperative that any strategies that address women's offending and victimisation, such as both the *Female Offender Strategy* (2018) and the *Victims Strategy* (2018), acknowledge and address the relationship between a woman's domestic abuse victimisation and her offending.

Employment of Women-centred and Trauma-informed Approaches

Traditionally the explanations, motivations and needs of women who come into contact with the CJS have often been overlooked by a system that was developed by men, for men. The CJS has been designed to control male offenders and manage their needs and as a result women who come into contact with the CJS have been marginalised and mistreated. In recent years in the UK, in part due to the pioneering work of Corston (2007), increased attention has been paid to the particular vulnerabilities experienced by women within the CJS. Consequently, the prevalence of domestic abuse within the histories or backgrounds of women who have come into contact with the CJS has become an area of interest within UK-based policy relating to women's offending. Academic work in this area, however, has been scarce and prior to the research outlined in this book little attention has been paid to how a woman's experience of domestic abuse may influence or affect her pathway into crime, and in particular how such experiences may drive a woman's offending.

The findings of the study reinforce theorisation that women have distinct criminogenic needs as they have different reasons for becoming involved in crime and their journeys into the CJS are significantly divergent from men's. The research findings therefore clearly indicate the need to recognise both the gendered pathways into offending and the specific needs of women who have offended, which includes recognition of, and support to address, histories of trauma and victimisation. Importantly, given the social commentary aspect of the findings of this research the outcomes wholly support the following statement that:

> Most of the solutions to women's offending lie outside of prison walls in treatment for addictions and mental health problems, protection from domestic violence and coercive relationships ... address[ing] the causes of [women's] offending. (PRT, 2014b, n.p.)

Implications for Policy and Practice – Recommendations

> The link that frequently exists between women's experiences of domestic violence and sexual abuse and their offending behaviour, should be taken into account when designing local service provision for women victims and offenders. (Earle et al., 2014, p. 5)

It should always be remembered that the findings of the study outlined in this book are based upon the real-life experiences of women and therefore the recommendations arising from it have real-world implications. As a result it is important to apply research findings to the real world and 'bridge the gap' between theory and practice (Skinner et al., 2005). The importance of using research to inform both policy and practice is further reinforced when the feminist approach taken for this study employed is considered. The importance of discussing the real-world implications of the study aligns with the feminist perspective that value should be allocated to ensuring that women's voices are amplified as well as acknowledged by practitioners and policy makers (Skinner et al., 2005).

Prior to, and after the completion of this research, appeals have been made for criminal justice services to recognise domestic abuse as a driver to women's offending, where this should consequently be addressed within both the design and delivery of services for women coming into contact with the CJS (see PRT, 2017a, 2014a; Roberts, 2016; Earle et al., 2014; Women's Aid, 2011). These calls have been accompanied by the rationale that in order to establish meaningful and targeted initiatives to address the roots causes of women's involvement in crime, their re-offending and, most importantly, their criminalisation, the motivations and explanations for the pathways women take to become engaged with the CJS must be both acknowledged and addressed.

Implications for the Probation Service

As a consequence of undertaking research within a criminal justice setting, as well as involving criminal justice professionals in the research itself, there are a range of recommendations arising from the research that relate to the supervision and support of women who come into contact with the CJS who have experienced domestic abuse. The findings of the study also have implications for a wider range of criminal justice professionals including those working within the police and court services and a range of these recommendations will be outlined below.

Specialist Domestic Abuse Training

Given the prevalence of domestic abuse within the backgrounds and histories of women who come into contact with the CJS it is imperative that those supervising and supporting women have an in-depth understanding of domestic abuse. As has been demonstrated, a woman's experience of domestic abuse can influence her pathway into crime, her ability to comply with her community-based sentence and opportunities to desist from crime. Therefore, having a better understanding of domestic abuse could help inform sentence and safety planning, the development and delivery of services/forms of support for women who come into contact with the CJS, desistence strategies and policies for better supporting women offenders. If a woman's experience of domestic abuse has been instrumental in her involvement in crime then identifying the appropriate support that she may need to address the domestic abuse may also address possibilities of re-offending.

Also, given that policy and legislation in the area of domestic abuse (and wider forms of violence against women) has developed considerably in recent years (for example with the addition of coercive control to the statutory definition of domestic abuse, with 16 and 17 years old being added and the introduction of the Domestic Abuse Bill in 2021) any professionals receiving training on domestic abuse should have regular access to refresher training. Most importantly, as it is those who work in specialist frontline support who are the experts in the field, they are best-placed to deliver any domestic abuse training to criminal justice practitioners.

As has been proposed earlier in the book it would be helpful to develop specific training which includes the following:

- Awareness raising: understanding the whole range of abusive behaviours that constitute domestic abuse and coercive control.
- How domestic abuse victimisation can impact upon women's pathways into crime.
- How a woman's experience of domestic abuse can impact upon her ability to comply with a community-based sentence.
- How a woman's experience of domestic abuse can impact on desistence.

Pre-sentence Reports

The study has emphasised how the process of conducting a pre-sentence report provides one of the only opportunities to understand how a woman has come into contact with the CJS and how her life experiences may have influenced her journey. As a consequence there are strong arguments for only full-delivery reports to be produced for all women about to be sentenced. Given the prevalence of domestic abuse victimisation in the histories of many women who come into contact with the CJS, there is a clear need for PSRs to include routine enquiry into women's relationships, experience of domestic abuse and more specifically questions relating to how women's experiences of domestic abuse may have contributed to their offending.

Making Domestic Abuse Awareness Courses Available to Women Who Come into Contact with the CJS

Many of the women who took part in the study who had been subjected to domestic abuse were not aware of the full range of abusive behaviours, particularly in relation to behaviours outside of physical violence. Coercive control, emotional/psychological and financial abuse were the elements of abuse that were less well-recognised. If women were able to access training or workshops which raise awareness of the whole range of forms of domestic abuse and what healthy relationships look like this could contribute to their well-being. Not only this but given a woman's experience of domestic abuse can, in some cases, impact upon her ability to comply with her sentence this could also help compliance.

The Importance of Women-only Reporting

The findings of this study highlight the importance of women-only reporting as providing spaces from which men are excluded helps to address some of the barriers that women who have been subjected to domestic abuse can face when attempting to carry out their sentences. Barriers include women being accompanied to probation visits by abusive partners, feeling intimidated by male-dominated environments or coming into contact with an abusive ex-partner. One further key aspect of women-only reporting, which related to the specific way in which it was implemented by the Wales Probation Trust at the time of the study, was the provision of specialist support services for women to access at the time they report to probation. The types of services which are important for women who have been subjected to domestic abuse to be able to access include domestic and sexual violence services, counselling, substance use, and financial support services. Given the often-chaotic nature of women's lives and the control they may be subjected to by abusive partners the provision of support services delivered in a one-stop-shop style can enable women to access much needed services which would not be possible should separate journeys to those services be needed. Women-only reporting also aligns with a more gender responsive and trauma-informed approach to the supervision of women serving sentences in the community as it acknowledges the impact victimisation can have upon women's engagement with probation. Not only can initiatives like this have positive outcomes for women's well-being but also for the probation service if it supports women in their ability to comply.

Providing Women-only Options for Court-mandated Requirements/ Conditions When Sentencing

Providing women-only options for court-mandated requirements or conditions may help alleviate some of the problems associated with women's ability to comply when they continue to experience domestic abuse whilst serving their sentence in the community. As with women-only reporting, the provision of an environment that may be less traumatic for women, and equally would not cause any problems for women when confronted by a controlling partner, may aid their compliance. To provide just one example; the option of women-only substance misuse programmes are specifically relevant as women's substance misuse may be employed as a coping mechanism for their experiences of domestic abuse, as a result it is not simply the substance use that needs to be addressed it is domestic abuse which functions as the root cause.

Implications for the Court Service

Training

It is not just those working for the Probation service that would benefit from training on domestic abuse, it is important that any criminal justice professional coming into contact with women should also have an understanding of how domestic abuse can impact upon a woman's pathway into crime. It is therefore imperative that Magistrates, who often have the most contact with female offenders, are well-informed of the various ways that women's experiences of domestic abuse may have influenced their involvement in crime. Furthermore, as there are a wide range of negative repercussions which arise from the sentencing decisions made by those in the court service both Magistrates and Judges may find value in training on the implications of particular sanctions for women who have been subjected to domestic abuse. Furthermore, other criminal justice professionals associated with the court process such as barristers and solicitors should also be well-informed about the root causes of their clients' involvement in crime as they may be able to be drawn upon for mitigation.

The Importance of PSRs

As noted in the section above PSRs are a highly valuable mechanism for collecting information about the background to women's offending. Sentencers should therefore ensure that wherever possible the necessary time is provided for full-delivery reports to be produced for all women being sentenced.

Sentencing

As highlighted in the chapter on professional perspectives (Chapter 10) sentencing decisions made by the judiciary can have significant implications for women who have experienced, or continue to experience domestic abuse when attempting to complete their sentence in the community. As a result, there are two areas that should be considered by sentencers.

Up-tariffing.   The professional perspectives chapter identified the highly inappropriate practice of up-tariffing where the severity of the sentences enforced by Magistrates or Judges reflect women's support needs rather than the actual crime committed. Any form of up-tariffing, whether that be enforcing a custodial sentence to remove a woman from an abusive relationship or adding additional requirements to account for women's additional support needs, should be avoided. Despite the intention sentencers may have for up-tariffing it is a highly problematic practice which can cause additional and often long-term problems for women and their children, particularly where imprisonment is part of the sentence. Sentencers should always consider the range of disposals available to them including diversionary pathways, community-based interventions and the involvement of specialist support services as an alternative to criminalising often extremely vulnerable and traumatised women where their involvement in the CJS can further traumatise and victimise them.

Awareness of the Effects of Particular Sanctions for Female Offenders who are Victims of Domestic Abuse.   A further area of concern highlighted in the professional perspectives chapter demonstrated that certain sanctions allocated by sentencers can have particularly difficult consequences for women who have come into contact with the CJS and are still being subjected to domestic abuse. In particular curfew, tag, and the imposition of fines were identified as problematic as they may put women at further risk of domestic abuse or cause them to encounter further problems with the law. As a result sentencers should be aware of the impact that particular sanctions may have upon women including, for example, when imposing a curfew may confine a woman to a house she shares with an abusive partner putting her at increased risk. In addition, when setting bail conditions/licence conditions or order requirements is the address that the woman is registered to live safe (for example does she live with her abusive partner?). Alternatively is her allocated accommodation safe (female only or with male offenders who could be contacts of her abuser?) Home circumstances checks could be incredibly beneficial for any women being sentenced by the court where the sanction involves something related to her housing provisions. Furthermore, if a woman's offending is financially motivated and could be the result of financial abuse is the imposition of a fine the appropriate sanction? It is imperative that sentencers consider the implications of the sanctions that they are going to enforce.

Other Recommendations

Women whose offending has been driven by domestic abuse should have access to diversion schemes and a wider range of community-based disposals should be available to them. There needs to be wider availability of women-only, gender responsive, trauma-informed community-based solutions for women who have experienced domestic abuse and become involved in crime to access.

There also needs to be a legal provision for an effective defence for women where their involvement in crime has been clearly driven by their domestic abuse victimisation (or indeed for any involvement in crime driven by any form of violence against women).

Final Words

Attempting, in some way, to subvert the oppression and imbalance of power that women are subjected to via their experiences of domestic abuse the voices of the women who participated in the study were placed at the very centre of the discourse. Consequently, the foundations of this book are built upon women's real-life experiences, which have real-world implications reinforcing the feminist notion that the personal is political. The value and strength of the research lies in the bravery and honesty of the women who took part emphasising the importance of applying research to the real world, bridging the gap between theory and practice and the need for women's perspectives to be better heard and addressed by policy makers and professionals working in the field of criminal justice.

As has been clearly demonstrated by the women's experiences, being subjected to domestic abuse can have a wide-ranging and long-term impact upon women's lives which can extend to bringing them into contact with the CJS as both victim and offender. Given the high volume of women with histories of domestic abuse victimisation who come into contact with the CJS, only by considering how the actions and strategies women employ to resist, cope with, or respond to these experiences can meaningful and appropriate interventions be developed for them. As this book has clearly evidenced it is essential that women's widespread experiences of victimisation must be both acknowledged and responded to using a women-centred and trauma-informed approach. If the root causes of women's pathways into crime are not acknowledged, and appropriately acted upon, the CJS will remain responsible for the continued criminalisation, re-victimisation and disempowerment of women, in many cases causing already traumatised women, and in some cases their children, further harm.

Appendices

Appendix A – Theoretical Positioning

The research outlined in this book drew upon a combination of two distinct but complementary theoretical perspectives, feminism and symbolic interactionism, and this section will briefly explain this choice.[1]

Feminist Epistemologies

The primary motivation for employing a feminist approach for this research was that the study focus was women, their lived experiences and their own accounts of their behaviour and actions. Consequently, the research adhered to Humm's (1995, p. 242) perspective of what feminist research should look like which is: 'grounded in the actual experiences and language of women's lives and experience in their own terms'. The gendered nature of domestic abuse, where being female is the single most significant risk factor (ONS, 2021, 2020a, 2020b; HMICFRS, 2019; HMIC, 2014; Refuge, 2014; Chaplin et al., 2011), as well as the gendered pathways into offending (MOJ, 2020; Prison Reform Trust, 2017a, 2017b; Silvestri, 2016), further explain and justify the feminist positioning of the study. The approach taken is further reinforced given female offenders' disparate treatment within the CJS and their disproportionate experiences of trauma and abuse (see Centre for Social Justice, 2018; Women in Prison, 2017; Prison Reform Trust, 2017a; and Jones, 2008) both of which demonstrate the need to employ a feminist perspective in order to understand how such gendered experiences may have influenced women's pathways into the CJS.

In contrast to traditional criminological research which has largely been produced by men, for men and has studied the criminal activities of men (see Stanley and Wise, 1990 and Heidensohn, 1985), the choice of employing a feminist perspective was symbolic as it aided the subversion of this aforementioned 'male gaze'. This deliberate rejection of the 'male gaze' was enabled by the research being produced by me as a female researcher, solely focussing on the perspectives and experiences of women. A further feminist facet of the study was that it also attempted to challenge the 'silencing effect' of domestic abuse (see Hague and Mullender, 2005) via providing a platform for women's voices to be heard. Without listening to the accounts of women who have experienced domestic abuse and become involved in crime it is impossible to understand the relationship between the two. Diverging from the already existing quantitative studies which highlight

---

[1]The content in this section has been condensed for brevity but is based upon a broader discussion of the ontological and epistemological positioning of the research which can be found in Roberts (2015). If you would like to explore the theoretical perspectives, why they were chosen and how they impacted upon the research design and practice in further detail see Roberts (2015, chapter 3.2).

the prevalence of women involved with the CJS who have experienced domestic abuse, this research instead provided a qualitative insight into women's behaviours and actions. Instead of examining the statistical pervasiveness of the abuse and trauma experienced by women in the CJS this study sought out women's own accounts of their pathways into crime, asking them to provide their own analysis of how such experiences had affected them, therefore addressing a significant gap in the literature. Furthermore, by subverting both the androcentric focus of traditional criminological research and the 'silencing effect' of domestic abuse, an attempt was made to empower, not exploit, the women who took part in the study. Providing women with a platform to amplify their voices was also highly significant given their experiences of abuse which often suppress, or totally deny, women the ability to explain and contextualise their actions. Feminist epistemologies also assert the need to recognise that those who are directly affected by social phenomena like domestic abuse are best placed to articulate how these experiences have affected and impacted them (see Rollins, 1985), hence the need to place the women's own perspectives and voices at the very centre of the discourse.

It should of course be recognised that feminism as a perspective it not monolithic, as the label 'feminist' acts as an umbrella term to describe a myriad of approaches. It is therefore important to recognise the differences that exist both within feminism as a perspective and between women as individuals (see Stanley and Wise, 1990). Women do of course experience a collective oppression, facilitated by a patriarchal society which creates and reinforces unequal power relationships between men and women[2] (Comack, 2000) yet within this wider social context each woman will experience her life individually and differently. Therefore, although the study recognises the significant impact that a woman's position in society will have upon her behaviour and actions (macro-perspective) it is imperative that each woman's individual experiences and how they respond to their domestic abuse victimisation (micro-perspective) are recognised. Therefore, it is important to note that:

> trying to unravel all of the factors which might be relevant [to women's offending] is no small order ... nevertheless, there is one factor in particular which stands out: the centrality of abuse in the women's lives. (Comack, 2000, p. 12)

As a consequence, it is necessary to examine the effect of gender, and women's collective experience of oppression, on women's pathways into crime.

Symbolic Interactionism

As the preceding paragraph suggests, using a feminist approach as a singular perspective upon which to build the research would not have been sufficient. It is

---

[2]At this point it is also important to reference the concept of intersectionality and recognise how multiple forms of oppression, as well as women's social and political identities/categorisations such as, but not limited to, social class, race and sexuality, intersect and affect women's lives.

important to acknowledge that not all women who experience domestic abuse will commit crime and, most significantly, each abusive relationship will be experienced differently due to its highly personal and subjective nature. As a result, structural factors such as women's often subordinate position within a male dominated society, cannot be applied in isolation to explain how a woman's experience of domestic abuse may affect her involvement in crime. Feminism as a perspective cannot reveal how a woman's subjective and personal experience of domestic abuse may impact upon her own individual actions and behaviours. Therefore, although a patriarchal society provides a mechanism through which abusive relationships are enacted and reinforced, each woman in an abusive relationship will react differently, responding to the individual dynamics of that relationship. As a consequence, it is important to investigate both the macro and micro processes that, in combination, contribute to women's pathways into crime when experiencing domestic abuse. Or as Stark (2007, p. 194) suggests in his work on coercive control, there needs to be recognition that:

> [...] each household governed by coercive control, each relationship, becomes a patriarchy in miniature, complete with its own web of rules or codes, rituals of deference, models of enforcements, sanctions and forbidden places.

As a result there is a distinct need to acknowledge and examine the subjective and individualised contexts in which women experience domestic abuse. The need to take such a perspective is further reinforced given domestic abuse is often enacted in the private sphere of the home and the dynamics of domestic abuse are informed by and derive from the personal knowledge an abuser has about his victim and the privileged access he has to her (Stark, 2007). All of this information provides justification for employing a symbolic interactionist perspective which allows for an idiographic focus on a woman's individualised experience of domestic abuse accompanied by an in-depth, interpretive, exploratory investigation of how such experiences can impact upon a woman's behaviour and actions.

Symbolic interactionism[3] views human–social interaction as a subjective process where people allocate specific 'meanings' to their interaction with one-another and these 'meanings' are produced via an interpretive social process (Blumer, 1986). The application of symbolic interactionism within this study therefore allowed for an analysis of the interaction between abuse perpetrator and victim and the meanings allocated to their interactions which subsequently affected the woman's involvement in crime. Using a symbolic interactionist perspective provided a mechanism through which the subjective, personal, and highly specific meaning which is attributed to the gestures and interactions between the perpetrator and victim of domestic abuse could be understood. How domestic abuse victims interpret the actions, gestures, and behaviours of their perpetrators

---

[3]Symbolic interactionism is a term coined by Blumer (1986) and as a social theoretical framework, it focusses upon the ways in which humans attach meanings to events and phenomena via their interaction with each other.

shapes their responses to this abuse and the resultant behaviour is often highly idiosyncratic and situationally specific. In addition, the meaning associated with the interaction between domestic abuse perpetrator and victim is often only understood by those involved in the relationship. The way in which someone *outside* of this relationship may interpret the same behaviour and gestures can be extremely different to how the victim of domestic abuse does (see Anderson, 2009 and Stark, 2007). An example of this is provided in Stark's (2007) book which details how 'Cheryl', a victim of domestic abuse, would respond to her partner's gesture of giving her his sweatshirt. When this happened Cheryl's friends noticed that she would '..."fall apart"' (Stark, 2007, p. 229). Stark (2007) elaborates:

> Cheryl's [friends] interpreted Jason's gesture as caring. But to Cheryl, the message was that she had violated an agreement not to make him jealous. The sweatshirt was his warning that, because of her infraction, she would have to cover up her arms after he beat her. (p. 229)

This provides a clear example of the symbolic interaction between an abuse perpetrator and abuse victim where the correct meaning of the behaviour can only be understood by those involved in the relationship as Cheryl's abuser's actions are interpreted very differently by those outside of the relationship.

In conclusion, the feminist and symbolic interactionist perspectives complement each other in that they acknowledge how both structural factors, which create and reinforce unequal power relations between abuse perpetrator and victim, and individual actions taken within an abusive relationship combine to influence and affect women's behaviours and actions. Therefore, this combination of perspectives allows for an analysis that recognises '... a gendered social process with distinct, individual-level, identity-based dimensions and dynamics' (Anderson, 2009, p. 1446). Consequently, this partnering of theoretical perspectives facilitates a more holistic approach to understanding how a woman's experience of domestic abuse may influence her pathway into crime via the bridging of macro and micro theory and sociological and psychological perspectives.

Translating Theory into Practice

It is important to note that feminist scholars assert that when a feminist approach is employed it should not only be present within the theoretical foundations of research, it should also filter through into the practicalities of the research processes (see Stanley and Wise, 1990 and Mulvey, 1988). As Mulvey (1988) in particular asserts, feminist studies should be characterised by feminist values and practice where the research processes align with those feminist values, as the two are unequivocally connected. As a consequence, the theoretical and epistemological positioning adopted for this study also influenced the research design, methods employed and the analytical approach taken, illustrating how theory can be directly translated into research practice. A range of examples of the ways in which the theoretical positing of the study influenced the research design and processes will be outlined in the following sections.

Appendix B – Research Design

Research Purpose

Female offenders are far more likely to have experienced domestic abuse than the wider female population (Centre for Social Justice, 2018; Women in Prison, 2017; Prison Reform Trust, 2017a; Women's Aid, 2011; Jones, 2008), yet despite wide recognition that many female offenders have histories of abuse, prior to the study outlined in this book there was a lack of research attempting to understand *how* a woman's experience of abuse may affect her pathway into crime. The purpose of this study was therefore to explore the relationship between a woman's experience of domestic abuse and her involvement in crime primarily to investigate ways in which such experiences may have *influenced* or *affected* the woman's pathway into offending. The study subsequently focussed upon the ways in which women cope with, respond to, or resist being subjected to domestic abuse and how such actions could impact upon their involvement in crime.

The vast majority of existing literature in this field had focussed upon women in prison, a minority demographic unreflective of the wider population of women involved with the CJS.[4] To address this, the research detailed in this book instead focussed upon women serving their sentences in the community as they comprise the majority of women who have been convicted of a criminal offence.

Research Methods

Qualitative Approach

A predominantly qualitative approach was employed for this study and this was for numerous reasons. First, at the time the research was undertaken the vast majority of existing literature in the UK which acknowledged a relationship between a woman's experience of domestic abuse and her pathway into crime comprised of quantitative data and the literature was largely policy-based (see, e.g., Prison Reform Trust, 2014a; MOJ, 2013b, 2012a; NOMS, 2008 and HMCIP, 1997). Existing data highlighted the prevalence of domestic abuse victimisation within the histories and backgrounds of women involved with the CJS, therefore suggesting that a relationship between a woman's experience of domestic abuse and her involvement in crime exists. There were, however, very few studies which had attempted to explain and analyse *how* this relationship actually operates – which was the focus of the study outlined in this book. A qualitative approach was adopted as quantitative data does not contextualise or provide insight into the reasons *why* so many women involved with the CJS have been subjected to domestic abuse nor does quantitative data help explain women's motivations for offending/the pathways they took to become involved in the CJS. Consequently,

---

[4]The most recent figures from the MOJ indicate that as at the 30 September 2021 there were 3,199 women in custody (MOJ, 2021b) compared with 21,291 women being supervised by Probation Services as at June 2021 (MOJ, 2021c).

a qualitative approach was most appropriate for this research as it enabled the women involved in the study to allocate meaning and provide a context to their actions and behaviours and therefore shed light upon the interaction between their experience of domestic abuse and their involvement in crime.

Second, the design and implementation of the study itself cannot be separated from the theoretical positioning therefore the methods employed for the study had to complement the feminist and symbolic interactionist approach. Hence the tools selected for the study were clearly linked to, explained and justified by the theoretical standpoint. Feminist epistemology is often immediately linked to a qualitative research design (Oakley, 2000) as feminists argue that qualitative methods allow for a better reflection of women's experiences, thoughts and interactions (see Humm, 1995), however, a number of considerations were made when designing the study, related to both the theoretical and practical elements of the research. It is also important, at this stage, to state that when describing a qualitative approach there is no single, one-dimensional design and there is of course huge diversity in reference to the paradigms, methods, and practices employed across the whole gamut of qualitative research (Punch, 2005).

In-depth Semi-structured Interviewing

Drawing upon the combined theoretical approach employed for the study the primary focus of the research was women, their lived experiences and their own analysis of their behaviour and actions therefore in-depth semi-structured interviewing was chosen as the most suitable data collection method. In contrast to closed, structured interviewing, semi-structured interviewing can be perceived to enable a more feminist approach as this method functions more as a guide, providing the women involved in the study with more control over the interview process. In addition, semi-structured interviewing was also specifically chosen as an attempt to address the power imbalance that exists between researcher and researched so that I as a researcher could transfer power to the research participants via providing as much room for the participants to steer and shape the content of the interview as possible and the ability to discuss subjects they felt were most important.[5]

Furthermore, semi-structured interviewing facilitated exploration of the women's *own* views of reality and the meanings they allocated to their own behaviours and actions allowing them to contribute to and produce theory (rather than myself as a researcher alone), again another technique to address the power hierarchies in research practice. Therefore, rather than prescribing existing theoretical concepts upon the women involved in the study due to the flexible data collection method the interview schedules were amended as the research progressed allowing

---

[5]Attempting to address any researcher/research participant power imbalance was doubly significant within this study given the power imbalance and abuse experienced by the women within their abusive relationships and it was imperative that the women retained as much control over the research process as was possible.

for the women's answers, theories, and perspectives to impact directly upon both the direction of the research and the subsequent findings arising from it. It should of course be acknowledged that the ability to transfer power is limited and it is unlikely that the unequal power dynamics involved in research practice can ever be fully eradicated (Maynard, 1994).

In-depth semi-structured interviewing also strongly aligns itself with symbolic interactionism as it allows for investigation of how individuals construct their own realities in reference to the interaction they have with others (both people and structures). An exploratory, investigate approach therefore reinforced the symbolic interactionist perspective of the study enabling an understanding of the structural factors which create and reinforce coercive and controlling behaviours and domestic abuse whilst recognising them as 'a gendered social process with distinct, individual level, identity-based dimensions and dynamics' (Anderson, 2009, p. 1446). Therefore, this method facilitated insight into the women's personal and individualised interpretation of the events, behaviour, gestures and relationships, which led them into their contact with the CJS.

Sampling

Over a period of seven months a total of 42 interviews were completed with both women involved in the CJS and a range of staff working for, what was then, the Wales Probation Trust.[6] The total number of individuals who took part in the study was 40 and this was divided into interviews with 25 women who were involved with the CJS (to elaborate; at the time of the study the vast majority of the women who participated had been convicted of a criminal offence and were either currently serving/or had recently completed a sentence under the supervision of the Wales Probation Trust). A supplementary sample of 15 professionals employed by the Wales Probation Trust were also interviewed for the research. To explain the additional two interviews; one woman involved with the CJS was interviewed twice, as was one of the probation staff. The second interview was required for the woman involved with the CJS as she wished to end the first interview and resume at a later date due to the difficulties she experienced when attempting to concentrate for prolonged amounts of time. In regard to the practitioner, the interview was split over two different days simply because the time she had initially allocated for the interview did not allow her to complete all the interview questions.

The number of completed interviews reflect the range of practical challenges that arose during the fieldwork of the study namely the implicit sensitivities of

---

[6]The fieldwork for the research took place prior to the implementation of the Ministry of Justice's *Transforming Rehabilitation* (MOJ, 2013a) after which, on the 1 June 2014, the Wales Probation Trust ceased to exist and was instead replaced by the National Probation Service (NPS) Wales and the Wales Community Rehabilitation Companies (CRC). Subsequently, in June 2021 after order from the Government the National Probation Service was reunified and all CRC contracts ended. In Wales sentence management was unified in December 2019.

researching two particularly taboo areas and issues of 'gatekeeping' by some probation staff members all of which is elaborated upon in Roberts (2015). Despite some challenges in recruiting the necessary number of research participants a wealth of data was acquired.

Primary Sample: Women Involved with the CJS Who Had Experienced Domestic Abuse

The primary sample was comprised of 25 women who had been convicted of a criminal offence and who defined themselves as having experienced domestic abuse. The vast majority of the women were recruited via the Wales Probation Trust (23) and a much smaller number of women (2) were recruited via Llamau which is a charity that works with young people and vulnerable women to end homelessness in Wales. At the time of the fieldwork the women that were recruited via Probation were either in the process of completing a sentence in the community and being supervised by Probation or had recently completed their community-based sentence. All of the women interviewed defined themselves to be White British or Irish[7] and were aged between 22 and 54. The offences that the women had committed varied significantly and are detailed in the table below.

Primary Sample Table: Women Involved with the CJS

Pseudonyms are used to refer to all of the women involved in the study to ensure they would remain anonymous. Another practical application of the study's feminist approach included giving the women an option to choose their own pseudonyms, as an attempt to empower them and involve them in the research process. Where women chose not to select a pseudonym, with their permission, one was selected for them.

---

[7]Unfortunately it was not possible to recruit a more diverse research sample. All women were asked to volunteer their participation in the study and although different social classes were represented, as well as a range of age groups, no black or minoritised women volunteered to take part. The absence of any black or minoritised women from the study could reflect the smaller number of black or minoritised people that live in Wales and the even smaller number of black or minoritised women being supervised by the Wales Probation Trust at the time of the study. Black or minoritised individuals comprised around four percent of the total population of Wales (Campbell, 2014) and at the time of the research, April 2012–March 2013, black or minoritised women comprised only 3.9 percent of the total number of women being supervised by the Wales Probation Trust (data provided directly from the Wales Probation Trust). Alternatively, or additionally, the lack of black or minoritised women could suggest that they may have experienced other barriers to becoming involved in the research such as language barriers, the type of abuse being experienced (such as so-called honour-based violence) which may restrict women's movements if being monitored by extended family or black or minoritised ethnic women may not wish to discuss their experiences with a white British researcher.

Woman Involved in the CJS (pseudonym)	Age	Offence[8]	First Offence?	Relationship History[9]	Substance Use?
Donna	30	Perverting the course of justice	No	2 abusive relationships disclosed. Duration: 1st boyfriend 7 years, 2nd boyfriend 6.5 years.	Alcohol
Charlie–Ann	28	Having an article with a blade in a public place – Malicious wounding (and other like offences)	Yes	3 abusive relationships disclosed. Duration: 1st boyfriend 5 years, 2nd ex-husband 18 months, 3rd on/off partner length of relationship unclear.	Alcohol and drugs
Cathy	41	Arson endangering life	Yes	Multiple abusive relationships disclosed. Childhood abuse by father continuing into adulthood, domestic abuse from ex-husband and multiple boyfriends over a number of years. Adolescent to parent violence (APV) also identified and perpetrated by her son.	Alcohol and drugs
Ellie	21	Burglary non-dwelling (that would be other premises)	Yes	2 abusive relationships disclosed. Duration: 1st boyfriend 4.5 years Current (at time of interview) familial abuse from sister.	Alcohol and drugs
Summer	34	Robbery and Assault with Intent to Rob	Yes	2 abusive relationships disclosed. Duration: 1st relationship 2 years, 2nd relationship 7 years.	Alcohol and drugs

(*Continued*)

Woman Involved in the CJS (pseudonym)	Age	Offence[8]	First Offence?	Relationship History[9]	Substance Use?
May	48	Common Assault	No	Multiple abusive relationships disclosed. Duration: 1st ex-husband 7 years 2nd ex-husband 1.5 years 3rd male partner 4 years.	Alcohol
Dara	23	Malicious wounding	No	2 abusive relationships disclosed. Duration: 1st boyfriend 6 years, 2nd boyfriend 7 months.	Drugs
Jo	45	Driving after consuming alcohol or taking drugs	Yes	3 abusive relationships disclosed. Duration: 1st ex-husband 7 years, 2nd ex-husband 4 years, 3rd ex-partner 2 years.	Alcohol
Sian	31	Social Security Offences (Benefit Fraud)	Yes	3 abusive relationships disclosed. Duration: 1st boyfriend 4 years, 2nd ex-husband 8 years, 3rd boyfriend 1.5 years.	Drugs
Linda	54	Driving or attempting to drive whilst unfit through drink	Yes	1 abusive relationship disclosed. Duration: male partner 6 years.	Alcohol
Margaux	40	Stealing from Shops and stalls (shoplifting)	No	Multiple abusive relationships disclosed (more than 3). Duration: 1st relationship 1.5 years, length of the remaining relationships unclear.	Drugs

Name	Age	Offence		Relationship	Substance
April	44	Assault on a police officer	Yes	1 abusive relationship disclosed. Duration: ex-husband 15 years.	None
Robin	36	Possession of class A drugs (heroin)	No	1 abusive relationship disclosed. Duration: male partner 4 years.	Drugs
Skye	23	Aggravated Burglary non-dwelling	No	1 abusive relationship disclosed. Duration: boyfriend 1 year.	Drugs
Mary	44	Common and Other types of Assault	Yes	1 abusive relationship disclosed. Duration: ex-husband 20 years.	Alcohol
Cece	30	Handling stolen goods	No	2 abusive relationships disclosed. Duration: 1st boyfriend 9 years, 2nd male partner (current at time of interview) 3 years.	Alcohol and drugs
August	27	Cruelty or Neglect of Children	Yes	2 abusive relationships disclosed. Duration: 1st male partner 3.5 years, 2nd male partner 5 years.	Drugs
Ida	42	Wounding and other acts of endangering lives	Yes	2 abusive relationships disclosed. Duration: 1st relationship 7 years, 2nd relationship on/off for 4 years.	Drugs
Charlie	28	Imprisonment – migrated breaches	No	Multiple abusive relationships disclosed. Duration: Unclear as interview had to be stopped.	Drugs
Nancy	45	Stealing by an employee	Yes	1 abusive relationship disclosed (APV experienced from son). Duration: First identified problems with her son when he was 7 (age at time of interview 24).	None

(Continued)

Woman Involved in the CJS (pseudonym)	Age	Offence[8]	First Offence?	Relationship History[9]	Substance Use?
Alana	38	Cruelty to or neglect of children	Yes	1 abusive relationship disclosed. Duration: 4.5 years.	Drugs
Grace	49	Fraud – Dishonest representation for obtaining benefit (benefit fraud)	Yes	1 abusive relationship disclosed. Duration: 25 years.	None
Violet	33	Supplying or offering to supply class B drugs	No	2 abusive relationships disclosed. Duration: Raped by an acquaintance and Male partner 2 years.	Drugs
Shayan	38	Assault occasioning ABH	No	1 abusive relationship disclosed. Duration: 11 years.	None
Cindy	43	Section 20 GBH/ Wounding	Yes	2 abusive relationships disclosed. Duration: 1st relationship 2 years, 2nd relationship 7/8 years	Drugs

[8] The offences referenced in the table are those offences that the women were serving their sentence for at the time of their interview/the most recent offence for which they had completed their sentence.

[9] The relationships detailed in the table are those that were disclosed by the women and labelled as abusive by them. It is important to note that I also perceived some of the additional relationships that the women discussed as abusive whereas the women themselves did not. It is important to note the disparity between what the participants and I viewed as/perceived to be abusive which could perhaps relate to minimisation, denial, and/or labelling. It was also sometimes difficult to ascertain how long relationships had lasted as multiple experiences of abuse were disclosed and the women's narratives would move from past to present making it difficult to distinguish how long relationships had lasted.

Supplementary Sample: Probation Service Staff Members

The supplementary sample was composed of fifteen professionals all of whom worked for the Wales Probation Trust and were based within five different Local Delivery Units (LDUs) across Wales covering both urban and rural locations. The vast majority of professionals interviewed were Probation Officers (POs) or Probation Service Officers (PSOs); the main distinction between the two roles is that PSOs supervise lower risk offenders than fully qualified POs. The sample did also include four professionals working in other roles including middle management, project or research-based work, and strategic roles. The years of service completed by the professionals also varied from 18 months to 32 years and many of those interviewed had specific expertise in the field of domestic abuse or held additional responsibilities specifically related to female offenders.

Interestingly, all of the staff interviewed for the research were women, although this was not something that was stipulated when the staff were recruited to the study. This could reflect the fact that the vast majority of those working in probation as POs/PSOs and those with an expertise in female offending and/ or domestic abuse are women. It could also reflect probation practice at the time whereby it was generally female POs/PSOs, as opposed to male POs/PSOs that were allocated women to supervise.

It should also be noted that during the course of the fieldwork and interviewing a number of the professionals also disclosed that they themselves had been victims of domestic abuse. This is unsurprising given the prevalence of domestic abuse and may explain why these particular individuals wished to participate in the research.

Supplementary Sample Table Two: Probation Service Staff Members.

Practitioner Number	Years of Service (Years)	Type of Position/Level of Seniority
1	15	Probation Officer with experience of working in the courts
2	1.5	Research Officer with prior experience as a Probation Officer
3	4.5	Probation Officer with experience of courts work, programmes, and victim support work
4	12	Probation Officer
5	32	Probation Officer with specific domestic violence responsibilities
6	11	Probation Officer and team manager with specific female offender responsibilities
7	9	Recently qualified Probation Officer with experience of role with specific female offender responsibilities
8	11	Probation Officer with courts experience
9	28	Team Manager, formerly with specific domestic violence responsibilities
10	19	Team Manager with some specific domestic violence responsibilities
11	8	Probation Officer with specific female offender responsibilities
12	7.5	Probation Officer with specific female offender responsibilities
13	2.8	Probation Officer with experience of working within the third sector in a domestic violence role
14	10	Probation Services Officer
15	10	Strategic Role with experience of working as Probation Officer

Appendix C – Ethical Considerations and Approvals

Given the implicit sensitivities of conducting research with a particularly vulnerable group, women who were survivors of domestic abuse and involved in the CJS, there were a substantial number of ethical considerations involved in the theoretical positioning, design, and practicalities of the study. When producing research on sensitive topics, as Sieber (1993) contends, ethics are of paramount importance due to the consequences involvement in the study can have for those participating in it. Therefore, the primary ethical consideration related to this study was ensuring that the participants were able to give informed consent to their involvement. When designing a study, it is important to be aware of, and adhere to, the ethical guidelines provided by the particular association linked to your academic discipline. In this case the British Sociological Association (2002) guidelines were followed to ensure the interests of any prospective participant were upheld and that the findings of the research were reported accurately and truthfully.

There are of course particular sensitivities associated with researching domestic abuse and researchers such as Downes, Kelly, and Westmarland (2014) have suggested that researching the different forms of violence against women can involve complicated ethical dilemmas specifically relating to the safety of both participants and their families. In studies exploring forms of violence against women it is imperative to understand that the participants' involvement in the research can have direct implications for their safety and in some cases can lead to a threat against their lives being made by the perpetrators of the abuse (see WHO, 2005). The well-being and safety of research participants should always take precedence therefore the gravity of the dangers involved with conducting research on domestic abuse and other forms of violence against women should not be understated. Given the particular sensitives associated with researching domestic abuse, however, further and more specialised guidance was also followed (see WHO, 2005, 2001[10]). When considering the well-being of those involved in research it is also important to incorporate the needs of the researcher.

Ethical approvals were received from multiple committees and individuals to ensure the fieldwork for the study could take place. Ethical approvals were granted by the University of Leicester College of Social Sciences Ethics Committee, from the Chief Executive of the Wales Probation Trust, the Wales Probation Trust Practice and Performance Committee[11] and from the Director of Operational Services at Llamau.

---

[10]Since the completion of the doctoral research outlined in this book more recent guidance has been published – see WHO (2016).

[11]The Practice and Performance Committee was comprised of senior/managerial staff from the Wales Probation Trust as well as academics and professionals from external institutions and this committee oversaw any research being undertaken within the Trust.

Informed Consent

Central to any research project is the protection of the rights of the participants (see Noaks and Wincup, 2004) as a result informed consent should be a prerequisite to any research involving human participants. Informed consent can be summarised as the process which ensures those taking part in the study do so freely after being given full information regarding what it means for them to take part. Consent must be received before prospective participants take part in any aspect of the research. Given that all of the women who took part in the research had experienced domestic abuse and therefore had been subjected to coercive or controlling behaviours, informed consent was of increased importance as it was imperative that none of the women felt in any way pressurised into taking part. Several processes were implemented during the study to ensure true informed consent was achieved and these processes included:

- Emphasising the participants' right to withdraw from the study at any time without explanation;
- Providing all prospective participants with a briefing sheet that included content which: outlined the purpose of the study, who (as a researcher) I was, that participation would be anonymous and confidential (with certain exceptions), what taking part would entail and what the research would be used for. This was provided in writing to all participants and in some cases, due to participant literacy, was read in its entirety to the participant.

Care was taken to ensure that the language used in any communication with the women was accessible and participants were given the opportunity to ask questions at all stages of the study.

It was decided from the beginning of the study that it would be made absolutely explicit to participants that they would be asked to talk about their experiences of domestic abuse. It was considered imperative that all those invited to take part understood exactly what they would be asked about. Every effort was taken to avert any harm or distress that the study may invoke for those taking part as a result of recollecting upsetting and traumatic experiences and there were many women who did wish to take part but felt unable to talk about painful or distressing memories that, at the time they were invited for interview, they felt were too raw.

There were also several stages to the consent process and I met with all participants to ensure informed consent had been achieved. Until the point that informed consent had been achieved and the consent form signed, no interviews were booked in.

Vulnerability of Research Participants and Informed Consent

A quick note regarding the vulnerability of women who have experienced domestic abuse: although the women that were interviewed for this study could be viewed as vulnerable, as a result of their victimisation and involvement in the CJS, it was thought that they *were* in a position to provide informed consent. Downes et al. (2014) state that there are problems with labelling survivors of abuse as inherently vulnerable within research practice as, contrastingly, their experiences of domestic abuse could instead increase their alertness to potential threats and consequently heighten their ability to make decisions about taking part in a process which may cause them distress or harm. This theory is corroborated by the difficulties experienced in recruiting participants for this particular study,[12] a challenge which itself illustrates that survivors will and do exercise their agency by deciding not to participate in the research at all.

Safety and Protection from Harm

The United Nations (2012) advocates the need to take special care when researching any form of violence against women and both the safety of participants during the research process as well as avoiding causing participants any further harm as a result of their involvement must be considered. Speaking about experiences of domestic abuse can illicit extremely emotional responses and it can be traumatising for individuals to re-live such painful and distressing memories (WHO, 2005). As a result specialist ethics and safety guidance for researching in the field of violence against women has been developed by the WHO and this guidance was adhered to throughout the study (see WHO, 2001, 2005).

One of the WHO's (2001) recommendations for researching in the field of violence against women is that those undertaking the research must have a clear and informed understanding of the risks involved with the research itself. Here my background was significant as I had worked in the field of domestic abuse for over 5 years prior to commencing my doctoral research,[13] therefore this provided a strong foundation to understanding the effects of domestic abuse, safety considerations for working with women who have experienced domestic abuse and the ability to appropriately risk-assess situations. As a result of the risks associated with women taking part in research about domestic abuse a range of considerations were reviewed and practically addressed in order to retain their safety including:

---

[12]Although a total of 50 women who had experienced domestic abuse and were being supervised by probation agreed to take part in the study there were 29 instances where women did not attend their scheduled appointment with me. There were of course a range of reasons for this including the sensitive subject matter, not being able to attend due to the control of an abusive partner or simply a reflection of the reality of the women's sometimes chaotic lives. Therefore, it was decided that a supplementary sample of probation staff members would be interviewed which consequently allowed for data triangulation via drawing upon the staff members' wealth of experience of supervising and supporting women serving community-based sentences.

[13]Prior to undertaking my doctoral research I had worked in a domestic abuse refuge, had completed postgraduate research with women living in refuge, had undertaken training on key risk assessment models in the field of domestic abuse and had also been employed in roles to strategically address domestic abuse. As a result I had established a reasonable level of knowledge about domestic abuse and how it can impact upon women and their children.

- The location of the interviews; women were interviewed in the probation offices or Llamau premises to provide them with a safe place. The interviews also took place at the time that the women would usually be reporting to probation, or meeting with their support worker, so as not to rouse the suspicions of any abusive partners if the women were in an abusive relationship at the time of their interview.
- Interviews were conducted on an individual basis in a private room, without anyone known to the woman present to retain confidentiality.
- The subject matter of the research was not widely promoted so it would not be obvious what the women would be meeting with me to talk about.
- A decision was made to exclude any women who were being discussed at MARAC from the study, this was to ensure that those at greatest risk of homicide were not put at any further risk through their involvement.
- Many of the women who took part in the study spoke about what had taken place in previous relationships and were no longer in abusive relationships at the time of their interviews which also mitigated the risk associated with taking part in the study significantly.

Supporting Participants During and After the Research

It is important to recognise that individuals who take part in research, particularly research discussing traumatic experiences, may require support after the interviewing/study is over, but it is not the role of the researcher to provide such support. For this study it was an ethical imperative to ensure that all women who took part were offered information about how to access specialist, free support should they wish to do so after the interviewing was completed and the study had come to an end. Information was therefore supplied to all women who participated in this study regarding how to contact, what was then the All-Wales Domestic and Sexual Violence Helpline.[14] The helpline number and contact information was chosen as it was a national number which could signpost callers to the most appropriate existing services in the woman's local geographical area. Information about the helpline was offered to the women in the form of a credit card-sized information card, the size of which allowed the women to easily hide the card on their person should this be necessary. Of course not all of the women interviewed for the study were still in abusive relationships and therefore did not accept the information given to them and in some cases women did not feel that they needed the information provided.

There is a wealth of literature focussing on the negative elements of researching domestic abuse which is fortunately accompanied by guidance to prevent any negative experiences for participants and researchers. In contrast to the possible negative impact that research into violence against women may have, however, if conducted sensitively and in a supportive manner there can be positive outcomes

---

[14]This service has been replaced with the Live Fear Free helpline and information about this service can be found here: https://gov.wales/live-fear-free (Welsh Government, 2022).

for those taking part. For example, the positive elements of studies in this field include the research process itself empowering women, giving them a voice where they may previously not have had one[15] and helping to affect changes arising from the women's discourses to improve policy and practice in order to help support other women. Some of the women who participated in this research spoke of the cathartic and positive effects being involved in the study had for them, as this statement from Charlie-Ann illustrates:

> It's nice to be able to actually be completely honest and let it out, and not [have a response like] 'you've done wrong by giving your kids away, or you've done wrong by this'. Do you know what I mean? It's nice not … you're not looking at me with disgust or anything, where anybody else would be. And I know I've made mistakes and I can't change them. I can only try to help 'em a little bit better for others in the future. (Charlie-Ann)

One of the most important elements of research in the field of domestic abuse is providing a supportive and non-judgemental environment which is what Charlie-Ann particularly appreciated. Notably, individuals taking part in research relating to trauma reporting that their participation has been a positive experience has been documented by multiple other academics demonstrating the value of applied research on violence against women (see DePrince and Chu, 2008; Cromer et al., 2006; Newman et al., 1999; Kelly, 1988).

Confidentiality and Anonymity

Confidentiality and anonymity are two concerns applicable to all forms of social research, however, when researching domestic abuse such concerns arguably have greater significance when much of the information shared is deeply personal and can have explicit implications for a woman's current and/or future safety (WHO, 2005). If an abuse perpetrator were to discover that his victim was taking part in a study about domestic abuse this could have life-threatening implications for them, hence both confidentiality and anonymity were of central concern during and after the research. Many of the women that participated in the research had left their abusive relationships and were recounting their experiences retrospectively, which mitigated the risks somewhat. Some of the women, however, were still in abusive relationships and steps had to be taken to ensure their safety (as outlined in the section above). Therefore, all women and probation staff were protected from identification within the research through the anonymization of interview transcripts and ensuring that any highly identifiable details were also removed. To protect participants from being identified within the research pseudonyms

---

[15]This is particularly relevant given the 'silencing effect' of domestic abuse and the levels of control exerted by perpetrators of abuse (see Hague and Mullender, 2005). It could be argued, however, that the women's participation in research and sharing their experiences and own perspectives subvert the silencing effect to some extent.

were allocated to each participant to protect their identities (see the next section, addressing power hierarchies, for further detail regarding the use of pseudonyms).

There were, however, some instances where a woman's confidentiality could not be upheld due to both legal and ethical implications. As with any similar research, it was explained to all participants that confidentiality could not be retained after interview if during the interview the women disclosed information which led me to believe that the participant or someone else referenced in the interview, such as the participant's children, were at any significant risk of harm.

Addressing Power Hierarchies

Aligned with the feminist foundations of the research attempts were made to address the imbalance of power involved in the research process itself and in particular the power structures related to the relationship between myself as a researcher and the research participants (or 'subjects' as sometimes referred to outside of feminist literature). Oakley (1988) suggests that the power imbalance between researcher and research participant can be subverted via the researcher disclosing or sharing personal experiences as part of the research process (or, as she describes it, the interviewer investing their own 'personal identity' into the researcher/researched relationship). Oakley's approach was implemented during the fieldwork for the study as all participants were given the opportunity to ask me questions about myself prior to the interview (with no restrictions regarding the content of those questions). This process therefore attempted, in one way, to subvert the exploitative nature of the interview process where participants are viewed simply as a source of data (Maynard, 1994). Instead, this opportunity for information exchange gave the women involved in the study an opportunity to also be privy to personal information about someone else (this is especially relevant given the sensitive nature of the information the women themselves were being asked to disclose).

Another attempt to involve the women in as much of the research processes as possible and therefore continue to subvert the traditional power structures associated with the researcher/researched dynamic was made via the use of pseudonyms. Consistent with the feminist approach employed for the study when referring to the women who participated in the study it was decided that the use of the term 'Offender 1' or 'Offender 2', for example, was dehumanising. Instead, all of the women were given the opportunity to pick their own pseudonyms, a process attempting to further involve the women in the research process and empower them. Where women chose not to select their own pseudonym, with their permission, one was chosen for them.

Finally, providing a platform for the women's voices to be heard also, to some degree, subverts the 'silencing effect' of domestic abuse (Hague and Mullender, 2005) empowering, rather than exploiting, the women who participated in the study. It is, however, important to acknowledge that the transference of power facilitated through the research tools employed was limited, and it is unlikely that the unequal power dynamics that exist within research practice can ever be fully eradicated.

Appendix D – Data Analysis

All of the participants gave permission for their interviews to be audio recorded and subsequently transcribed. I took brief notes during the interviews themselves and immediately after interview as part of the reflective process (see Davies, 2000). These notes recorded any immediate thoughts upon the interview content and helped to establish any key themes or patterns arising from the women's narratives as the research progressed. This approach was taken as I believe analysis to be an ongoing process which starts at the interview stage and becomes more directional after all the interviews are completed, transcribed, and reviewed (see Gerson and Horowitz, 2002).

For this study I chose to transcribe the vast majority of interviews verbatim and did this myself as this process allowed me to be more immersed in the data and its meanings as well as enabling retention of the understanding of the nuances of the interaction and conversation that had taken place (see Davies, 2000). Towards the end of the transcription process I decided to pay a professional transcriber to complete the small number of remaining interviews. This decision was made in response to the emotive nature of the interview content and the process of having to repeatedly listen to upsetting and traumatic content for hours at a time.[16] Here it is perhaps important to pass comment on the impact of conducting research within the field of violence against women. It should be recognised that researching violence against women can take an immensely emotional toll, not only upon those recollecting their traumatic experiences but also upon those researching it. The WHO (2005, p. 41) support this statement as they identified that one of the most common risks for researchers in this field is the 'emotional toll of listening to women's repeated stories of despair, physical pain and degradation'. In the case of this study, the interviewing combined with transcription itself and the consequent process of 're-living' the women's experiences and often distressed or emotional recollections of the domestic abuse they had been subjected to contributed heavily to the emotional impact of completing this study. The concept of secondary trauma is of particular relevance here as this refers to the affects that indirect exposure to traumatic events via first-hand recollections or narratives can have on those researching areas such as violence against women. Other terms such as compassion fatigue (Figley, 1995) and vicarious trauma (Pearlman

---

[16]Transcribing the interviews was a challenging process for me due to listening to the women's recollections of disturbing and traumatic events, which were often recollected by the women in an emotional and distressed way. Listening to the women's accounts over and over again to ensure the women's words were captured and doing so over an intense time period allocated for the fieldwork proved to be a very emotional task. One of the emotions evoked by this process was guilt which transpired as a result of me asking the women to recount some of the worst and most traumatic experiences of their lives, something which I struggled with throughout the fieldwork. These feelings of guilt were mitigated somewhat by the gratitude that some of the women expressed for being listened to as well as the women's hopes that the outcomes of the research may help support women in similar positions to them.

and Saakvitne, 1995) are sometimes used interchangeably with secondary trauma generally to convey the theory that discussions of traumatising events can have an emotional impact not just upon those who have directly experienced the trauma and who are recounting this trauma but those who are bearing witness to such accounts. Regardless of terminology, however, secondary trauma has been widely recognised as something experienced by frontline professionals working in mental health and violence against women (as just two examples) and more recently some attention has been paid to the secondary trauma experienced by researchers in the field of violence against women and girls.[17] Any negative effects of the secondary trauma and feelings of guilt for asking the women to re-live distressing and traumatic experiences were, however, to a certain extent, remedied by firstly helping raise the women's voices and secondly by some of the gratitude expressed by the women for listening to their stories from a non-judgemental perspective. DePrince and Chu (2008), Cromer et al. (2006), Newman et al. (1999) and Kelly (1988) have also documented that taking part in trauma-based research can have some positive outcomes for participants.

An Inductive Approach

An inductive approach, of an exploratory and descriptive orientation, was employed for the data analysis involved in this study. The inductive approach applied comprised what is often referred to as a 'bottom-up' approach (see Braun and Clarke's, 2006, discussions of inductive versus deductive approaches) where the themes developed arise from and are closely related to the data itself. Unlike a deductive approach which attempts to fit the data collected to existing or pre-prescribed themes/ideas to prove or disprove hypotheses an inductive approach lets the data speak for itself. In the case of this study the purpose was to understand how, if at all, a woman's experience of domestic abuse could contribute to her pathway into crime therefore the themes arose from the women's own narratives and the themes were developed with no preconceived ideas about how this relationship manifested itself or indeed if there was any connection between them at all. This process shares similarities with grounded theory where concepts are grounded in the data itself as opposed to established prior to the research which then attempts to test an already existing hypothesis.

An inductive approach was also selected as this type of analysis is often favoured by feminist researchers (Mason and Stubbs, 2010) and consequently was deemed most appropriate given the feminist theoretical foundations of the research. The approach employed for this study aligns with feminist theoretical approaches to data analysis in that the themes emerged directly from the women's words and collective narratives taking into consideration the nuances and subjectivity of the women's individual experiences. This style of analysis keeps the

---

[17]For further discussions of the impact of secondary trauma upon researchers in the field of domestic abuse specifically see Williamson et al. (2020).

women's voices and experience at the very centre of the discourse, which was a vital aim of the study.

It is important to mention, however, that employing an inductive approach does not equate to an unproblematic mode of interpretation. As Braun and Clarke (2006, p. 84) note it is not possible to completely remove researchers' ideas from the analysis and development of themes as: 'researchers cannot free themselves of their theoretical and epistemological commitments, and data are not coded in an epistemological vacuum'. As a result a 'multivocality' (Snyder, 2008) is established where the multiple meanings of the women's experiences of victimisation, with the meanings the women themselves *and* the researcher have attached to their experiences are produced. Consequently, the women's words and experiences remain at the centre of the discourse but their experiences are translated into coherent themes and theory for an academic audience by the researcher (Mason and Stubbs, 2010).

Thematic Analysis

The style of data analysis employed within this study was thematic, which refers to a process of identifying descriptive 'themes', directly from the data itself, and developing concepts that were founded in the commonalties existing across the interviews with the women (as the primary focus of the study) which were often supported or further validated by the probation staff member interviews. Thematic analysis was chosen as it enabled an exploration of '…the ways in which events, realities, meanings, experiences and so on are the effects of a range of discourses operating within society' (Braun and Clarke, 2006, p. 81). In particular thematic analysis enabled an examination of the interaction between abuse perpetrator and survivor, the meanings allocated to the interaction by the woman being subjected to domestic abuse, where the actions and behaviours within the abusive relationship are often interpreted very differently by those outside of it. Hence the style of data analysis is heavily consistent with the symbolic interactionist perspective employed, as this type of analysis paid particular attention to the meanings and symbolism allocated to the women's actions by the women themselves.

Importantly, as the preceding paragraphs have demonstrated, thematic analysis although based heavily upon the words and accounts of the women goes further via the development of collective themes. Or as Braun and Clarke (2006, p. 84) explain:

> a thematic analysis at the latent level goes beyond the semantic content of the data, and starts to identify or examine the underlying ideas, assumptions, and conceptualizations – and ideologies – that are theorized as shaping or informing the semantic content of the data.

As a result the thematic approach comprises multiple levels of analysis moving beyond the words alone, interpreting meaning rather than being purely descriptive and instead develops theories or concepts from the repeated patterns of meaning established across the discourses of those involved in the research (Braun and Clarke, 2006).

The decision was also made not to undertake any form of computer-aided data analysis which again was as a result of the theoretical approach adopted for the study. Due to wishing to study the very micro-dynamics of the women's abusive relationships it was felt that special attention needed to be paid to the women's language and specific words they used as well as the subjective nature of the meanings the women attributed to their recollections of events. Therefore, for this reason, computer-aided analysis was deemed unsuitable as this process would have arguably diluted the opportunity to focus more acutely on the women's narratives, their choice of words and their analysis of their behaviours and actions within their own subjective contexts. In addition, it was also felt that the use of computer software was ill-fitting of the feminist approach to the study as computer software is often aligned with a positivist, masculinist, data-processing culture (Stroh, 2000) which strongly contrasts with the subjective, woman-centred, and narrative-focussed approach employed in this study.

References

Abrahams, H. 2007. *Supporting Women After Domestic Violence: Loss, Trauma and Recovery*, London, Jessica Kingsley.

Abrahams, H. 2010. *Rebuilding Lives After Domestic Violence: Understanding Long-term Outcomes*, London, Jessica Kingsley.

All Party Parliamentary Group on Women in the Penal System. 2020. *Briefing Two: Arresting the Entry of Women into the Criminal Justice System*, London, The Howard League for Penal Reform.

Anderson, K.L. 2009. Gendering coercive control, *Violence Against Women*, 15(12), 1444–1457.

Australian Law Reform Commission. 2017. *Pathways to Justice – An inquiry into the Incarceration Rate of Aboriginal and Torres Strait ISLANDER PEOPLES. ALRC Final Report 133*. Sydney, Australian Law Reform Commission.

Australia's National Research Organisation for Women's Safety. 2020. *Women's Imprisonment and Domestic, Family, and Sexual Violence: Research Synthesis*. ANROWS Insights, 03/2020. Sydney, NSW, Australia's National Research Organisation for Women's Safety.

Barrett, M.R., Allenby, K. and Taylor, K. 2010. *Twenty Years Later: Revisiting the Task Force on Federally Sentenced Women. Report No. R-222*. Ottawa, ON, Correctional Service Canada.

Barry, M. and McIvor, G. 2010. Professional decision making and women offenders: containing the chaos?, *Probation Journal*, 57(1), 27–41.

Becker, S. and McCorkel, J. 2011. The gender of criminal opportunity: the impact of male co-offenders on women's crime, *Feminist Criminology*, 6(2), 79–110.

Bindel, J. 2018. Women who kill their partners are still being treated differently to men, *The Guardian*. Available at: https://www.theguardian.com/commentisfree/2018/jul/10/women-kill-partners-men-emma-humphreys-abused [Accessed 4 August 2021].

Bloom, B., Owen, B. and Covington, S. 2014. Women offenders and the gendered effects of public policy. In *Women and Crime: A Text/Reader*, Ed. S. Mallicoat, 2nd ed., pp. 477–491, London, Sage.

Blumer, H. 1986. *Symbolic Interactionism: Perspective and Method*, London, University of California Press.

Braun, V. and Clarke, V. 2006. Using thematic analysis in psychology, *Qualitative Research in Psychology*, 3(2), 77–101.

British Sociological Association. 2002. *Statement of Ethical Practice for the British Sociological Association*, Belmont, British Sociological Association.

Browne, A. 1987. *When Battered Women Kill*, New York, NY, The Free Press.

Browne, A. and Williams, K.R. 1989. Exploring the effect of resource availability and the likelihood of female-perpetrated homicides, *Law and Society Review*, 23, 75–94.

Carlen, P. 1983. *Women's Imprisonment*, London, Routledge and Keegan Paul.

Carlen, P. 1998. *Sledgehammer: Women's Imprisonment at the Millennium*, London, Macmillan.

Carlen, P. Ed. 2002. *Women and Punishment: The Struggle for Justice*, Cullompton, Willan.

Carlen, P. and Worrall, A. 2004. *Analysing Women's Imprisonment*. Cullumpton, Willan.

Centre for Social Justice. 2018. *A WOMAN-CENTRED APPROACH: Freeing Vulnerable Women From the Revolving Door of Crime*, London, Centre for Social Justice.

Centre for Women's Justice. 2021. *WOMEN WHO KILL: How the State Criminalises Women We Might Otherwise Be Burying*, London, Centre for Women's Justice.

Chaplin, R., Flately, J. and Smith, K. 2011. *Crime in England and Wales 2010/11: Findings from the British Crime Survey and Police Recorded Crime*, 2nd ed., London, Home Office.

Chesney-Lind, M. 1989. Girl's time and women's place: toward a feminist model of female delinquency, *Crime and Delinquency*, 35, 5–29.

Chesney-Lind, M. and Rodriguez, N. 1983. Women under lock and key: a view from the inside, *The Prison Journal*, 63, 47–65.

Comack, E. 2000. *Women in Trouble: Connecting Women's Law Violations to Their Histories of Abuse*, Halifax, Fernwood.

Corston, J. 2007. *The Corston Report: A Review of Women with Particular Vulnerabilities in the Criminal Justice System*, London, Home Office.

Council of Europe. 2011. *Council of Europe Convention on Preventing and Combating Violence Against Women and Domestic Violence 2011*. Available at: https://wcd.coe. int/ViewDoc.jsp?id=1772191 [Accessed 1 June 2012].

Craven, P. 2005. *The Freedom Programme: A Training Manual for Facilitators*, Wallasey, The Freedom Programme.

Cromer, L.D., Freyd, J.J., Binder, A.K., DePrince, A.P. and Becker-Blease, K. 2006. What's the risk in asking? Participant reaction to trauma history questions compared with reaction to other personal questions, *Ethics and Behavior*, 16(4), 347–362.

Crown Prosecution Service. 2019. *Violence Against Women and Girls Report 2018–19*. Available at: https://www.cps.gov.uk/sites/default/files/documents/publications/cps-vawg-report-2019.pdf [Accessed 12 January 2022].

Davies, P. 2000. Doing interviews with female offenders. In *Doing Criminological Research*, Eds V. Jupp, P. Davies and P. Frances, pp. 82–96, London, SAGE.

DeHart, D. 2004. *Pathways to Prison: Impact of Victimization in the Lives of Incarcerated Women*, Columbia, The Center for Child & Family Studies.

Department of Justice. 2010. *Women's Offending Behaviour in Northern Ireland: A Strategy to Manage Women Offenders and Those Vulnerable to Offending Behaviour 2010–2013*, Belfast, Department of Justice Northern Ireland.

DePrince, A.P. and Chu, A. 2008. Perceived benefits in trauma research: Examining methodological and individual difference factors in responses to research participation, *Journal of Empirical Research on Human Research Ethics*, 3(1), 35–47.

Dobash, R.P. and Dobash, R.E. 2004. Women's violence to men in intimate relationships. Working on a puzzle, *British Journal of Criminology*, 44(3), 324–349.

Domestic Abuse Act. 2021. Available at: https://www.legislation.gov.uk/ukpga/2021/17/contents/enacted [Accessed 12 January 2022].

Domestic Abuse Intervention Programs. 2011. *The Duluth Model: Power and Control Wheel*. Available at: http://www.theduluthmodel.org/pdf/PowerandControl.pdf [Accessed 20 February 2012].

Domestic Violence Information Manual. 1993. *The Duluth Domestic Abuse Intervention Project*. Available at: http://www.eurowrc.org/05.education/education_en/12.edu_en.htm [Accessed 27 February 2012].

Downs, W.R. and Miller, B.A. 1994. Women's alcohol problems and experiences of partner violence: a longitudinal examination. Paper presented at the annual meeting of the Research Society on Alcoholism, Maui, Hawaii.

Downes, J., Kelly, L. and Westmarland, N. 2014. Ethics in violence and abuse research – a positive empowerment approach, *Sociological Research Online*, 19(1). Available at: http://www.socresonline.org.uk/19/1/2.html [Accessed 12 January 2022].

Dutton, D. 2006. *Rethinking Domestic Violence*, Vancouver, University of British Columbia Press.

Dworkin, A. 1993. *Letters from a War Zone*, Brooklyn, Lawrence Hill Books.

Earle, J., Nadin, R. and Jacobson, J. 2014. *Brighter Futures: Working Together to Reduce Women's Offending*, London, Prison Reform Trust.

Farmer, M. 2019. *The Importance of Strengthening Female Offenders' Family and other Relationships to Prevent Reoffending and Reduce Intergenerational Crime*, London, MOJ.

Felson, R., Messner, S., Hoskin, A. and Deane, G. 2002. Reasons for Reporting and Not Reporting Domestic Violence to the Police, *Criminology*, 40(3), 617–648.

Ferraro, K. 2006. *Neither Angels Nor Demons: Women, Crime, and Victimisation*, Boston, Northeastern University Press.

Festinger, L. 1957. *A Theory of Cognitive Dissonance*, Evanston, Row, Peterson and Company.

Figley, C.R. 1995. Compassion fatigue as secondary traumatic stress disorder: an overview. In *Compassion Fatigue: Coping With Secondary Traumatic Stress Disorder in Those Who Treat the Traumatized*, Ed. C.R. Figley, pp. 1–20, New York, NY, Brunner-Routledge.

Gelsthorpe, L. 2004. Female offending: A theoretical overview. In *Women Who Offend*, Ed. G. McIvor, pp. 13–37, London, Jessica Kingsley.

Gelsthorpe, L. and Morris, A. Eds 1990. *Feminist Perspectives in Criminology*, Milton Keynes, Open University Press.

Gelsthorpe, L., Sharpe, G. and Roberts, J. 2007. *Provision for Women Offenders in the Community*, London, Fawcett.

Gerson, K. and Horowitz, R. 2002. Observation and interviewing: options and choices in qualitative research. In *Qualitative Research in Action*, Ed. T. May, pp. 199–224, London, SAGE.

Gilfus, M. 1992. From victims to survivors to offenders: women's routes of entry and immersion into street crime, *Women and Criminal Justice*, 4(1), 63–89.

Gilfus, M. 2002. *Women's Experiences of Abuse as a Risk Factor for Incarceration*. Available at: http://www.vawnet.org/applied-research-papers/print-document.php?doc_id=412 [Accessed 12 January 2022].

Gorde, M.W., Helfrich, C.A. and Finlayson, M.L. 2004. Trauma symptoms and life skill needs of domestic violence victims, *Journal of Interpersonal Violence*, 9(6), 691–708.

Gracia, E. 2004. Unreported cases of domestic violence against women: towards an epidemiology of social silence, tolerance, and inhibition, *Journal of Epidemiology and Community Health*, 58, 536–537.

Hague, G. and Mullender, A. 2005. Listening to women's voices: the participation of domestic violence survivors in services. In *Researching Gender Violence: Feminist Methodology in Action*, Eds T. Skinner, M. Hester and E. Malos, pp. 146–167, Cullumpton, Willan.

Harne, L. and Radford, J. 2008. *Tackling Domestic Violence: Theories, Policies and Practice*, Maidenhead, Open University Press.

Hedderman, C. and Barnes, R. 2015. Sentencing women: an analysis of recent trends. In *Exploring Sentencing Practice in England and Wales*, Ed. J. Roberts, pp. 93–117, Basingstoke, Palgrave Macmillan.

Heidensohn, F. 1985. *Women and Crime*, Basingstoke, Macmillan.

Heidensohn, F. 1989. *Crime and Society*, New York, NY, New York University Press.

Heidensohn, F. 1996. *Women and Crime*, 2nd ed., Basingstoke, Macmillan.

Heidensohn, F. and Gelsthorpe, L. 2007. Gender and crime. In *The Oxford Handbook of Criminology*, Eds M. Maguire, R. Morgan and R. Reiner, pp. 381–421, Oxford, Oxford University Press.

Her Majesty's Chief Inspector of Prisons. 1997. *Women in Prison: A Thematic Review*, London, Home Office.

Her Majesty's Government. 2010a. *Call to End Violence Against Women and Girls: Action Plan*, London, HM Government.

Her Majesty's Government. 2010b. *Call to End Violence Against Women and Girls: Strategic Vision*, London, HM Government.

Her Majesty's Inspectorate of Constabulary. 2014. *Everyone's Business: Improving the Police Response to Domestic Abuse*, London, HMIC.

Her Majesty's Inspectorate of Constabulary. 2015. *Increasingly Everyone's Business: A Progress Report on the Police Response to Domestic Abuse*, London, HMIC. Available at: https://www.justiceinspectorates.gov.uk/hmicfrs/wp-content/uploads/increasingly-eve ryones-business-domestic-abuse-progress-report.pdf [Accessed 12 January 2022].

Her Majesty's Inspectorate of Constabulary and Fire and Rescue Services. 2019. *The Police Response to Domestic Abuse: An Update Report*, London, HMICFRS. Available at: https://www.justiceinspectorates.gov.uk/hmicfrs/wp-content/uploads/the-police-response-to-domestic-abuse-an-update-report.pdf [Accessed 12 January 2022].

Her Majesty's Inspectorate of Prisons. 2006. *Women in Prison: A Literature Review*, London, HMIP.

Hester, M. 2013. Who does what to whom? Gender and domestic violence perpetrators in English police records, *European Journal of Criminology*, 10(5), 623–637.

Hester, M., Pearson, C., Harwin, N. and Abrahams, H. 2007. *Making an Impact: Children and Domestic Violence A Reader*, 2nd ed., London, Jessica Kingsley.

Home Office. 2013. *Guidance: Domestic Violence and Abuse (Domestic Violence and Abuse: New Definition)*. Available at: https://www.gov.uk/domestic-violence-and-abuse [Accessed 16 April 2015].

Home Office. 2021. *Domestic Abuse Act Factsheet*. Available at: https://homeofficemedia.blog.gov.uk/2021/04/29/domesticabuseactfactsheet/ [Accessed 12 January 2022].

Humm, M. 1995. *The Dictionary of Feminist Theory*, 2nd ed., London, Harvester Wheatsheaf.

Humphreys, C. and Regan, L. 2005. *Domestic Violence and Substance Use: Overlapping Issues in Separate Services, Final Report*, London, Stella Project.

Humphreys, C. and Thiara, R. 2002. *Routes to Safety: Protection Issues Facing Abused Women and Children and the Role of Outreach Services*, Bristol, Women's Federation of England.

Inciardi, J., Lockwood, D. and Pottieger, A.E. 1993. *Women and Crack Cocaine*, New York, NY, Macmillan.

Jones, A. 1994. *Next Time She'll Be Dead: Battering and How to Stop It*, Boston, Beacon Press.

Jones, S. 2008. Partners in crime: a study of the relationship between female offenders and their co-defendants, *Criminology and Criminal Justice*, 8(2), 147–164.

Justice for Women. 2021. *Sally Challen*. Available at: https://www.justiceforwomen.org.uk/sally-challen-appeal [Accessed 4 August 2021].

Kaysen, D., Dillworth, T., Simpson, T., Waldrop, A., Larimer, M. and Resick, P. 2007. Domestic violence and alcohol use: trauma-related symptoms and motives for drinking, *Addictive Behaviours*, 32(6), 1272–1283.

Kelly, L. 1988. *Surviving Sexual Violence*, Cambridge, Polity Press.

Kelly, L., Sharp, N. and Klein, R. 2014. *Finding the Costs of Freedom: How Women and Children Rebuild Their Lives After Domestic Violence*, London: Solace Women's Aid and Child and Woman Abuse Studies Unit, London Metropolitan University.

Kirkwood, C. 1993. *Leaving Abusive Partners: From the Scars of Survival to the Wisdom for Change*, London, SAGE.

Kraft-Stolar, T., Brundige, E., Kalantry, S., Kestenbaum, J. and Avon Global Centre for Women and Justice at Cornell Law School and Women in Prison Project. 2011. *From

Protection to Punishment: Post-conviction Barriers to Justice for Domestic Violence Survivor–Defendants in New York State. Available at: http://scholarship.law.cornell. edu/avon_clarke/2 [Accessed 12 January 2022].

Krug, E., Dahlberg, L., Mercy, J., Zwi, A. and Lozano, R. 2002. *World Report on Violence and Health*, Geneva, World Health Organisation.

Lempert, L.B. 1996. Women's strategies for survival: developing agency in abusive relationships, *Journal of Family Violence*, 11(3), 269–289.

London Safeguarding Children Board. 2008. *Safeguarding Children Abused Through Domestic Violence*, London, London Safeguarding Children Board.

Malim, T. and Birch, A. 1998. *Introductory Psychology*, Basingstoke, Macmillan.

Malloch, M. and McIvor, G. Eds 2012. *Women, Punishment and Social Justice: Human Rights and Penal Practices*, Abingdon, Routledge.

Marougka, M. 2018. *Responding to the Needs of Women in the Criminal Justice System: Evaluation of the Training Delivered to Criminal Justice Professionals*, London, Together for Mental Wellbeing and Prison Reform Trust.

Mason, G. and Stubbs, J. 2010. Feminist approaches to criminological research, *Sydney Law School Legal Studies Research Paper*, 10(36), 1–32.

Maynard, M. 1994. Methods, practice and epistemology: the debate about feminism and research. In *Researching Women's Lives from a Feminist Perspective*, Eds M. Maynard and J. Purvis, pp. 10–26, London, Taylor and Francis.

McIvor, G. 2004. *Women Who Offend*, London, Jessica Kingsley.

McIvor, G. 2007. The nature of female offending. In *What Works with Women Offenders*, Eds R. Sheehan, G. McIvor and C. Trotter, pp. 1–22, Cullompton, Willan.

McWilliams, M. and McKiernan, J. 1993. *Bringing It Out in the Open: Domestic Violence in Northern Ireland*, Belfast, HMSO.

Ministry of Justice. 2012a. *A Distinct Approach: A Guide to Working with Women Offenders*, London, Ministry of Justice and National Offender Management Service.

Ministry of Justice. 2012b. *NOMS Commissioning Intentions for 2013–14: Discussion Document, July 2012*, London, Ministry of Justice and National Offender Management Service.

Ministry of Justice. 2013a. *Transforming Rehabilitation: A Strategy for Reform*, London, MOJ.

Ministry of Justice. 2013b. *Strategic Objectives for Female Offenders*, London, Ministry of Justice.

Ministry of Justice. 2013c. *Transforming Rehabilitation: A Summary of Evidence on Reducing Re-Offending* (*Ministry of Justice Analytical Series*), London, Ministry of Justice.

Ministry of Justice. 2018. *Female Offender Strategy*, London, MOJ.

Ministry of Justice. 2020. *Women and the Criminal Justice System. 2019*. Available at: https://www.gov.uk/government/statistics/women-and-the-criminal-justice-system-2019/women-and-the-criminal-justice-system-2019 [Accessed 13 June 2021].

Ministry of Justice. 2021a. *Pre-sentence Report Pilot in 15 Magistrates' Courts*. Available at: https://www.gov.uk/guidance/pre-sentence-report-pilot-in-15-magistrates-courts accessed 10th November 2021 [Accessed 12 January 2022].

Ministry of Justice. 2021b. *Prisons Data*. Available at: https://data.justice.gov.uk/prisons [Accessed 12 January 2022].

Ministry of Justice. 2021c. *Probation Data*. Available at: https://data.justice.gov.uk/probation [Accessed 12 January 2022].

Moe, A. 2004. Blurring the boundaries: women's criminality in the context of abuse, *Women's Studies Quarterly*, 32(3–4), 116–138.

Moloney, K.P., Van Den Bergh, B.J. and Moller, L.F. 2009. Women in prison: the central issues of gender characteristics and trauma history, *Public Health*, 123(6), 426–430.

Mulvey, A. 1988. Community psychology and feminism: tensions and commonalties, *Journal of Community Psychology*, 16, 70–83.

Myhill, A. 2015. Measuring coercive control: what can we learn from national population surveys?, *Violence Against Women*, 21(3), 355–375.

Myhill, A. 2017. Measuring domestic violence: context is everything, *Journal of Gender-based Violence*, 1(1), 33–44.

National Offender Management Service. 2008. *National Service Framework: Improving Services to Women Offenders*, London, Ministry of Justice and National Offender Management Service.

National Offender Management Service. 2013. *Stocktake of Women's Services for Offenders in the Community*, London, National Offender Management Service.

National Offender Management Service. 2015. *Better Outcomes for Women Offenders*, London, National Offender Management Service.

Newman, E., Walker, E.A. and Gefland, A. 1999. Assessing the ethical costs and benefits of trauma-focused research, *General Hospital Psychiatry*, 21(3), 187–196.

Noaks, L. and Wincup, E. 2004. *Criminological Research: Understanding Qualitative Methods*, London: SAGE.

Oakley, A. 1988. Interviewing women: A contradiction in terms. In *Doing Feminist Research*, Ed. H. Roberts, pp. 30–61, New York, NY, Routledge.

Oakley, A. 2000. *Experiments in Knowing: Gender and Method in the Social Sciences*, Cambridge, Polity Press.

Office for National Statistics. 2020a. *Domestic abuse in England and Wales Overview: November 2020*. Available at: https://www.ons.gov.uk/peoplepopulationandcommunity/crimeandjustice/bulletins/domesticabuseinenglandandwalesoverview/november2020 [Accessed 12 January 2022].

Office for National Statistics. 2020b. *Domestic Abuse Victim Characteristics England and Wales: Year Ending March 2020*. Available at: https://www.ons.gov.uk/peoplepopulationandcommunity/crimeandjustice/articles/domesticabusevictimcharacteristicsenglandandwales/yearendingmarch2020 [Accessed 17 March 2021].

Office for National Statistics. 2020c. *Statistical Bulletin: Domestic Abuse in England and Wales Overview November 2020*. Available at: https://www.ons.gov.uk/peoplepopulationandcommunity/crimeandjustice/bulletins/domesticabuseinenglandandwalesoverview/november2020 [Accessed 17 March 2021].

Office for National Statistics. 2021a. *Appendix Tables: Homicide in England and Wales*. Available at: https://www.ons.gov.uk/peoplepopulationandcommunity/crimeandjustice/datasets/appendixtableshomicideinenglandandwales [Accessed 12 January 2022].

Office for National Statistics. 2021b. *Domestic Abuse in England and Wales Overview: November 2021*. Available at: https://www.ons.gov.uk/peoplepopulationandcommunity/crimeandjustice/bulletins/domesticabuseinenglandandwalesoverview/november2021 [Accessed 12 January 2022].

Office for National Statistics. 2021c. *Domestic Abuse Victim Characteristics, England and Wales, Year Ending March 2021*. Available at: https://www.ons.gov.uk/peoplepopulationandcommunity/crimeandjustice/articles/domesticabusevictimcharacteristicsenglandandwales/yearendingmarch2021 [Accessed 12 January 2022].

Pearlman, L.A. and Saakvitne, K.W. 1995. *Trauma and the Therapist: Countertransference and Vicarious Traumatization in Psychotherapy with Incest Survivors*, New York, NY: W.W. Norton.

Pemberton, S., Balderston, S. and Long, J. 2019. *Trauma, Harm and Offending Behaviour: What Works to Address Social Injury and Criminogenic Need with Criminal Justice Involved Women? INITIAL FINDINGS*, Birmingham, University of Birmingham.

Prison Reform Trust. 2014a. *Transforming Women's Lives: Reducing Women's Imprisonment*, London, Prison Reform Trust.

Prison Reform Trust. 2014b. *Why Focus on Reducing Women's Imprisonment? A Prison Reform Trust Briefing*. Available at: http://www.prisonreformtrust.org.uk/Portals/0/ Documents/why%20focus%20on%20reducing%20womens%20imprisonment.pdf [Accessed 29 April 2015].

Prison Reform Trust. 2017a. *"There's a Reason we're in Trouble": Domestic Abuse as a Driver to Women's Offending*, London, Prison Reform Trust.

Prison Reform Trust. 2017b. *Why Focus on Reducing Women's Imprisonment? Prison Reform Trust Briefing*, London, Prison Reform Trust.

Prison Reform Trust. 2018. *What About me? The Impact on Children When Mothers are Involved in the Criminal Justice System*, London, Prison Reform Trust.

Punch, K. 2005. *Introduction to Social Research: Quantitative and Qualitative Approaches*, London, SAGE.

Radcliffe, P., Hunter, G. and Vass, R. 2013. *The Development and Impact of Community Services for Women Offenders: An Evaluation Research Report*, London, The Institute for Criminal Policy Research, School of Law, Birkbeck College.

Richie, B. 1996. *Compelled to Crime: The Gender Entrapment of Battered Black Women*, New York, NY, Routledge.

Refuge. 2014. The Gendered Nature of Domestic Violence – Facts and Figures. 2014. Available at: http://www.refuge.org.uk/files/Statistics-domestic-violence-and-gender. pdf [Accessed 26 February 2015].

Roberts, J. 2006. *The Links between Domestic Abuse and Women's Crime: A Preliminary Qualitative Investigation*. M.Sc. Econ Dissertation, Swansea, Swansea University.

Roberts, J. 2015. *'It Was Do or Die' – How a Woman's Experience of Domestic Abuse Can Influence Her Involvement in Crime: A Qualitative Investigation of the Experiences of Community-based Female Offenders*. PhD Thesis, Leicester, University of Leicester.

Roberts, J. 2016. *Identification of Community Based Female Offenders as Victims of Domestic Abuse*, Cardiff, Integrated Offender Management Cymru Women's Pathfinder Project.

Roberts, J., Her Majesty's Prison and Probation Service Effective Practice and Service Improvement Group. 2020. *7-Minute Briefing – Domestic Abuse as a Driver to Women's Offending*, London, HMPPS Effective Practice and Service Improvement Group.

Roberts, R. and Townhead, L. 2015. Punishing women and criminal justice failure. In *Empower, Resist, Transform: A Collection of Essays*, Eds H. Mills, R. Roberts, and L. Townhead, pp. 6–7, London, Centre for Crime and Justice Studies.

Rollins, J. 1985. *Between Women: Domestics and Their Employers*, Philadelphia, PA, Temple University.

Root, M. 1992. Reconstructing the impact of trauma on personality. In *Personality and Psychopathology: Feminist Reappraisals*, Eds L. Brown and M. Ballou, pp. 229–266, London, The Guilford Press.

Rumgay, J. 2004. *When Victims Become Offenders: In Search of Coherence in Policy and Practice*, London, Fawcett Society.

Safe Lives. 2021a. *Who Are the Victims of Domestic Abuse?*. Available at: https://safelives. org.uk/policy-evidence/about-domestic-abuse/who-are-victims-domestic-abuse [Accessed 12 January 2022].

Safe Lives. 2021b. *MARAC Data 2020–2021 England and Wales*. Available at: https://safe-lives.org.uk/node/2036 [Accessed 12 January 2022].

Schechter, S. 1982. *Women and Male Violence: The Visions and Struggles of the Battered Women's Movement*, Cambridge, South End Press.

Segrave, M. and Carlton, B. 2010. Women, Trauma, Criminalisation and Imprisonment ..., *Current Issues in Criminal Justice*, 22(2), 287–305.

Sieber, J. 1993. The ethics and politics of sensitive research. In *Researching Sensitive Topics*, Eds C. Renzetti and R.M. Lee, pp. 14–26, London, SAGE.

Silvestri, M. 2016. *Gender and Crime: A Human Rights Approach*, London, SAGE Publications.

Skinner, T., Hester, M. and Malos, E. 2005. Methodology, feminism and gender violence. In *Researching Gender Violence: Feminist Methodology in Action*, Eds T. Skinner, M. Hester and E. Malos, pp. 1–23. Columpton, Willan.

Smith, K.I. 2021. *The Femicide Census*. Available at: https://www.femicidecensus.org/ [Accessed 19 May 2021].

Smith, K., Coleman, K., Eder, S. and Hall, P. 2011. *Homicides, Firearm Offences and Intimate Violence 2009/10: Supplementary Volume 2 to Crime in England and Wales 2009/10, Second Edition*, London, Home Office.

Smith, K., Osborne, S., Lau, I. and Britton, A. 2012. *Homicides, Firearm Offences and Intimate Violence 2010/11: Supplementary Volume 2 to Crime in England and Wales 2010/11*, London, Home Office.

Snyder, R.C. 2008. What is third-wave feminism? A new directions essay, *Signs: Journal of Women in Culture and Society*, 34(1), 175–196.

Standing Together. 2021. *Multi-agency Risk Assessment Conference (MARAC)*. Available at: https://www.standingtogether.org.uk/marac [Accessed 11 December 2021].

Stanley, L. and Wise, S. 1990. Method, methodology and epistemology in feminist research processes. In *Feminist Praxis: Research, Theory and Epistemology in Feminist Sociology*, Ed. L. Stanley, pp. 20–60, London, Routledge.

Stark, E. 1999. A failure to protect: Unravelling "The battered mother's dilemma", *Western State University Law Review*, 27, 29–110.

Stark, E. 2007. *Coercive Control: How Men Entrap Women in Personal Life*, Oxford, Oxford University Press.

Stark, E. and Flitcraft, M. 1996. *Women at Risk: Domestic Violence and Women's Health*, Thousand Oaks, CA, SAGE.

Street, A., Gibson, L. and Holohan, D. 2005. Impact of childhood traumatic events, trauma-related guilt, and avoidant coping strategies on PTSD symptoms in female survivors of domestic violence, *Journal of Traumatic Stress* 18(3), 245–252.

Stroh, M. 2000. Computers and qualitative data analysis: to use or not to use …? In *Research Training for Social Scientists*, Ed. D. Burton, pp. 226–243, London, SAGE.

Social Exclusion Task Force. 2009. *Short Study on Women Offenders: May 2009*, London, Ministry of Justice.

Tam, K. and Derkzen, D. 2014. *Exposure to Trauma Among Women Offenders: A Review of the Literature. Research Report, R333*. Ottawa, ON, Correctional Service of Canada.

Task Force on Federally Sentenced Women. 1990. *Creating Choices*, Ottawa, Correctional Services of Canada.

Thompson, G. 2010. *Domestic Violence Statistics*, London, House of Commons Library.

United Nations. 1993. *Declaration on the Elimination of Violence Against Women*. Available at: http://www.un.org/documents/ga/res/48/a48r104.htm [Accessed 27 February 2012].

United Nations. 2012. *Virtual Knowledge Centre to End Violence Against Women and Girls*. Available at: http://www.endvawnow.org/en/articles/922-key-informant-interviews.html [Accessed 11 February 2014].

United Nations. 2013. *General Assembly, Sixty-Eighth Session: Pathways to, Conditions and Consequences of Incarceration for Women: Note by the Secretary-General (A/68/340)*. Available at: http://www.un.org/ga/search/view_doc.asp?symbol=A/68/340 [Accessed 6 August 2014].

United Nations Office on Drugs and Crime. 2014. *Handbook for Prison Managers and Policymakers on Women and Imprisonment*, Vienna, United Nations Office on Drugs and Crime.

Vickers, S. and Wilcox, P. 2011. Abuse, women and the criminal justice system, *Criminal Justice Matters*, 85(1), 24–25.

Violence Against Women, Domestic Abuse and Sexual Violence (Wales) Act 2015. Available at: https://www.legislation.gov.uk/anaw/2015/3/contents [Accessed 12 January 2022].

Walby, S. and Allen, J. 2004. *Domestic Violence, Sexual Assault and Stalking: Findings from the British Crime Survey*, London, Home Office Research, Development and Statistics Directorate.

Walby, S. and Towers, J. 2017. Measuring violence to end violence: mainstreaming gender, *Journal of Gender-based Violence*, 1(1), 11–31.

Walby, S. and Towers, J. 2018. Untangling the concept of coercive control: theorizing domestic violent crime, *Criminology and Criminal Justice*, 18(1), 7–28.

Walker, L. 1984. *Battered Woman Syndrome*, New York, NY, Springer.

Weare, S.F. and Barlow, C.F. 2019. Women as co-offenders: pathways into crime and offending motivations, *The Howard Journal of Criminal Justice*, 58(1), 86–103.

Welle, D. and Falkin, G. 2000. The everyday policing of women with romantic co-defendants, *Women and Criminal Justice*, 11(2), 45–65.

Welsh Government. 2022. *Live Fear Free Helpline*. Available at: https://gov.wales/live-fear-free [Accessed 12 January 2022].

Wilcox, P. 2006. *Surviving Domestic Violence: Gender, Poverty and Agency*, Basingstoke, Palgrave Macmillan.

Williamson, E., Gregory, A., Abrahams, H., Aghtaie, N, Walker, S.J. and Hester, M. 2020. Secondary trauma: emotional safety in sensitive research, *Journal of Academic Ethics*, 18, 55–70.

Women in Prison. 2017. *Corston +10: The Corston Report 10 Years On*, London, Women in Prison.

Women's Aid. 2011. *Supporting Women Offenders Who Have Experienced Domestic and Sexual Violence*, Bristol, Women's Aid Federation of England.

Women's Aid. 2021a. *Domestic Abuse Is a Gendered Crime*. Available at: https://www.womensaid.org.uk/information-support/what-is-domestic-abuse/domestic-abuse-is-a-gendered-crime/ [Accessed 12 January 2022].

Women's Aid. 2021b. *How Common Is Domestic Abuse?*. Available at: https://www.womensaid.org.uk/information-support/what-is-domestic-abuse/how-common-is-domestic-abuse/ [Accessed 12 January 2022].

World Health Organisation. 2002. *World Report on Violence and Health*, Geneva, World Health Organisation.

World Health Organisation. 2005. *Researching Violence Against Women: A Practical Guide for Researchers and Activists*, Washington D.C., World Health Organization.

World Health Organisation. 2016. *Ethical and Safety Recommendations for Intervention Research on Violence Against Women Building on Lessons from the WHO Publication: Putting Women First: Ethical and Safety Recommendations for Research on Domestic Violence Against Women*, Geneva, World Health Organisation.

World Health Organisation. 2021. *Violence Against Women*. Available at: https://www.who.int/news-room/fact-sheets/detail/violence-against-women [Accessed 4 November 2021].

Yamamoto, S. and Wallace, H. 2007. Domestic violence by law enforcement officers. In *Encyclopaedia of Domestic Violence*, Ed. N. Jackson, pp. 255–261, London, Routledge.

Index